THE

PUBLICATIONS

OF THE

SURTEES SOCIETY

VOL. CLXXXVIII

THE

PUBLICATIONS

OF THE

SURTEES SOCIETY

ESTABLISHED IN THE YEAR

M.DCCC.XXXIV

VOL. CLXXXVIII

FOR THE YEAR MCMLXXIII

At a COUNCIL MEETING of the SURTEES SOCIETY, held in Durham Castle on 2 June 1975, Mr. C. R. Hudleston in the chair, it was ORDERED—

"That the edition by Miss E. A. Playne and Mr. G. de Boer of Lonsdale Documents should be printed as a volume of the Society's publications."

A. J. Piper
Secretary.

LONSDALE DOCUMENTS

EDITED BY

ELIZABETH PLAYNE
AND
G. DE BOER

PRINTED FOR THE SOCIETY BY
NORTHUMBERLAND PRESS LIMITED
GATESHEAD
1976

CONTENTS

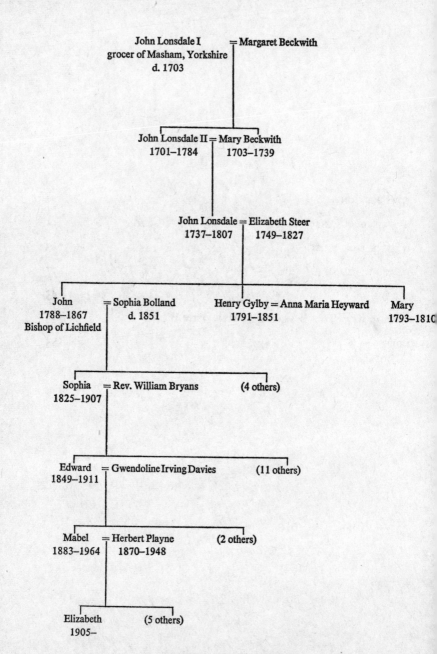

The Lonsdale family tree

INTRODUCTION

I. THE DOCUMENTS

The letters of the Rev. John Lonsdale printed here, though arranged in chronological order, fall into two groups. The first[1] consists of letters addressed by him to the Surveyor General or to his deputy, William Harrison, at the Land Revenue Office to further his efforts to secure a new lease of the Crown estate of Sunk Island in the River Humber, in which he had acquired an interest by marriage. The second is made up of the letters he wrote to his wife during the six months that he felt obliged to stay in London at a critical stage in the negotiations; these, as well as describing his personal thoughts and feelings on the progress of his application for a lease, touch on family matters.

These letters have remained in the possession of his descendants and are held at the present time by one of the authors of this introduction who is Lonsdale's great great great grand-daughter. They passed to her from her mother who had received them from an aunt whose mother, Sophia Bryans, was daughter of the Jack of the letters who later became Bishop of Lichfield. The ten letters which refer to the Bishop's boyhood and are thus of especial interest to the family had been separated from the remaining twenty-six which dealt with the Sunk Island lease and it was only in the course of transcription that it was realized that all thirty-six were written between February and July, 1779, during Lonsdale's prolonged stay in London. These private letters are dated informally and incompletely and their place in the sequence has often been determined by the postmark and from internal evidence.

This introduction therefore falls into two sections, one dealing with the Lonsdale family, the other with Sunk Island.

Printed also with these letters is the survey of Sunk Island made by William Whitelock 1797[2] in accordance with the requirements

---

[1] Public Record Office CRES/2/1446.
[2] P.R.O. CRES/39/60; University of Hull MS DRA 539.

of an Act of Parliament of 1794 that before a grant was made of a Crown estate there was to be a survey and valuation[3]. Whitelock's valuation and recommendation of further reclamation were of central importance in the negotiations.

[3] 34 Geo III, cap.75; see below, pp. 29-30.

II. THE LONSDALES

John Lonsdale (1737-1807), the writer of these letters, was born at Masham, Yorkshire in 1737. He was the son of John Lonsdale II (1701-84) who married in 1730 Mary (1703-39) daughter of William Beckwith of Lamb Hill. His grandfather, John Lonsdale I, a Masham grocer, married in 1698 Margaret, daughter of Michael Beckwith, a tailor of Nutwith Cote near Masham. According to an inscription in Masham church, John Lonsdale I died and was buried on 18 February 1703.

Until recent years there have been many Beckwiths associated with and living near Masham but no close connection appears between the Beckwiths of Nutwith Cote and those of Lamb Hill. Like John Lonsdale I, Michael Beckwith of Nutwith Cote was a tradesman but the Beckwiths of Lamb Hill appear to have been of a higher station in life, coming in 1656 from Ripon when Thomas Beckwith and his son bought the Lamb Hill estate.

John Lonsdale II appears to have been a person of property and influence in Masham. As early as 1730 his name occurs together with those of the churchwardens and other parishioners in a letter presented at the Visitation of the Dean and Chapter of York, protesting at the misdemeanours of the incumbent of Masham, the Rev. Peter Save. In 1741, in the Yorkshire contested election, John Lonsdale is included in the list of eleven Masham freeholders. In North Riding Deeds for 1740 and 1742 it is recorded that the Earl of Ailesbury and Elgin leased both land and a house to Lonsdale for 21 years. A deed of 1742 records that Lonsdale himself leased 7 acres of land. In 1769, 1781, and 1782, Lonsdale's name occurs with those of other Masham residents in the Land Tax returns. John Lonsdale was also a member of the Four and Twenty of Masham, an ancient body existing since the reign of Richard I and which, since 1662, appears to have had the sole charge of the oversight of the poor of the parish in addition to other duties including responsibility for church repairs. When he died in 1784, he was the last surviving trustee of land bequeathed in 1731 "for the most poor and impotent and aged people in the township of Masham", and held in trust by members of the Four and Twenty.

On the floor of the south side of Masham church is an inscription to "Mary, the wife of Mr. John Lonsdale of Masham and daughter of Mr. William Beckwith of Lamb Hill, buried September 20th 1739 aged 36 years. Also Mary her daughter, buried June 20 1740 aged 4 years".

Therefore John Lonsdale III, writer of the letters, lost his mother when he was only 2 years old and, after his sister's death a year later, was an only child. He was brought up in Masham and, in all probability, was often there until his father's death in 1784. As late as 1776, presumably when visiting his father, he officiated at a marriage in Masham church between Thomas Clark and Margaret Kay.

Many of the people referred to in the letters are either friends or the children of friends of Masham days who had gone to London. Chief among these were members of the Bolland family. On the west side of Masham church yard is a vault belonging to the Bollands of Masham where are buried John Bolland, for many years a respected inhabitant of the town who died in 1775, his wife Margaret, and six of his children. John Bolland was a shop-keeper combining, as was usual at that time, both the grocery and drapery business. Many of his large family went further afield and acquired both wealth and positions of some importance. One son, John Bolland, friend of the letter writer and often mentioned in the letters and whose daughter Sophia married John Lonsdale's elder son, the Jack of the letters, later Bishop of Lichfield, was an opulent hop merchant; he lived at Clapham Common and became M.P. for Bletchingley, Surrey. A grandson of John Bolland of Masham was Sir William Bolland, a successful lawyer who, in 1829 was created baron of the Exchequer and whose career is recorded in the Dictionary of National Biography.

It appears that during the years when John Lonsdale was growing up in Masham, it was a developing and prosperous place. In 1750 when John Lonsdale was a boy of 13, William Danby succeeded to the estate of Swinton in Masham parish and during his reign many improvements were made. He reclamation of moor-land attracted considerable attention and he was a substantial bene-factor to the charities of both church and town. He was also the largest contributor to the founding of the Grammar and Free

Schools. In 1768 when Arthur Young visited Masham he praised Danby's improvements highly especially commenting on the way the miners employed in the collieries on the edge of the moors were given small gardens and, if they cared for them well, were allowed to enclose and cultivate moorland.

William Bray, writing of Masham in 1777, says, "the market place of which is so uncommonly spacious built on three sides but the houses so low and mean that it has the appearance of a deserted place". A writer of 1865 thinks Bray's account exaggerated but quotes a verbal account he had had which told of how the houses were so low and the eaves of the thatched buildings nearly reached the ground so that at the September fairs, the sheep bounded and leapt on to the roofs of the houses and gambolled there presenting quite a spectacle to the beholder below.

Masham still has a spacious market place with houses on three sides, the church on the fourth and markets are still held there.

The first national census of 1801 gives Masham 2,520 inhabitants. The population appears to have been increasing. The recorded baptisms in 1740, three years after John Lonsdale's birth, were 30; in 1750 there were 51. In 1779 the boundaries of the parish included 22,525 acres of which 7,000 were moorland.

The beginning of a free school in Masham is first recorded in 1735 when Isabel Beckwith bequeathed £100 to be laid out in the purchase of lands for the benefit of a free school for the teaching of five poor boys to be selected by the Four and Twenty, preference to be given to those of the name of Beckwith. A further benefaction in 1748 increased the number of children but again stipulated that they should be of the poorest inhabitants of Masham. It therefore seems quite unlikely that John Lonsdale went to this school. We know that until 1757 he was a pupil at Queen Elizabeth's Grammar School at Wakefield; this school, founded in 1591, was then at the height of its fame. Dr. Thomas Zouch of Sandal Magna[1], a contemporary and friend of Lonsdale, writing at the end of the century says that the principal gentry of the county of York entrusted their sons to Thomas Clark, headmaster 1703-20, and the school had a high reputation. The next headmaster, Rev. Benjamin Wilson 1720-51, said to be the finest Greek scholar of his day, maintained the high reputation. Lonsdale's school days at Wakefield were mainly during the headmastership of the Rev. John Clark 1751-58

[1] Letter XV, n. 78.

who, during his time, is said to have sent out into the world a large number of men who became well known. In 1758 Lonsdale is named in a list of scholars and also among those who gave books to the library. In 1757 he was admitted pensioner of Trinity College, Cambridge, and in 1761 graduated as 3rd Senior Optime. Presumably he was ordained that same year as from 1761-68, he was curate at Bolsterstone in the Deanery of Doncaster, situated nine miles from Penistone and Barnsley. In 1768 Lonsdale became vicar of Darfield near Barnsley and in 1772 priest in charge of Chapelthorpe, a chapelry of Sandal Magna. These cures he held until his death in 1807. During this period he lived at Newmillerdam adjoining Chapelthorpe and about two miles from Wakefield.

When Lonsdale went to the parish in 1772 the old thirteenth-century church was no longer in existence. In 1770, the building had been in danger of collapse and a new chapel was built at a cost of £1,194, much of this sum having been raised by house to house collections. Lonsdale therefore inherited a new, though to judge from descriptions of it, far from attractive church building.

Whereas the stipend of the curate of Chapelthorpe only amounted to £11.6.2d. in 1705, grants from Queen Anne's Bounty in 1713 and 1735 and other benefactions had improved it and in 1751 a house at Hamley Moorside, near Newmillerdam with barn and stables was acquired as the minister's residence and there Lonsdale lived until his death.

In 1785 when he was 48 he was married in Scarborough to Elizabeth daughter of Charles Steer of Wakefield. After the birth of a daughter who died in infancy, a son John was born on 17 January 1788, another son, Henry Gylby, on 19 January 1791 and a daughter, Mary, on 18 November 1793; their baptisms are recorded in Sandal Magna church. Elizabeth (1749-1827), Lonsdale's wife, was a direct descendant of Anthony Gylby the first lessee of Sunk Island, and under the will of her uncle Robert Fretwell in 1791 received a share of one sixth of Sunk Island. The current lease, granted in 1771, was due to expire in 1802 and its renewal was the occasion of Lonsdale's six months stay in London in 1799 and it was during this period that the thirty-six letters to his wife were written. That Elizabeth was a woman of decided character and a business woman is clear from the letters. Her husband defers to her constantly and often gives way to her judgment in matters relating to the children as well as to the business in hand. It was she who filled in the income tax returns and, as 1799 was the first year of income tax, that can have been no easy task. She also had to cope with wages and decisions over the management of the glebe and she has left accounts of the cost of her son's schooling both at Heath and Eton. She outlived her husband by 20 years and, in her grand-daughter's reminiscences, is described as a clever old lady with a remarkable memory but a great coddle. She did not go out for many years but was always in bonnet and out of door wraps and was afraid to sit near a window, even when shut, in case she caught a cold. She lived in Wakefield and her son John took his wife and family posting to visit her. She was buried at Darfield in 1827.

Lonsdale appears to be in many respects a typical eighteenth-century parson. By the end of the eighteenth century there had become a great change in the social status of the clergy as can be seen by comparing the parsons in Fielding's novels and those of Jane Austen. The clergy were the first to emerge of a new professional class. The influence of the Evangelical Revival was probably partly responsible for this as it was also for the decline in non-residence and traffic in livings. Parson Woodforde, apart from some months in 1775, was always resident in his parish and only one of Jane Austen's parsons does not live in his. Lonsdale, however, appears to sit far more lightly to his parochial duties. In J. Walker's *History of Wakefield*, he is described as being largely non-resident and to have employed curates to do his work. From the letters, it appears there was only one curate to serve Darfield, some 12 miles off, and Chapel-thorpe, hence the difficulty over getting the duty done at Chapelthorpe during Lonsdale's long stay in London. Apart from the worry he caused his wife about arranging the Sunday duty, Lonsdale does not appear to have had any parochial cares and, after being away six months, even suggests going away with his wife to the sea when he returns. In the years 1799-1804 when he was actively concerned with the works on Sunk Island, he was more than ever an absentee parson.

Noticeably little space in Parson Woodforde's Diary is given to religion and all Jane Austen's parsons seem quite devoid of all spiritual function. It is the same with Lonsdale and in all his letters there is not one enquiry about any parishioner nor does he give any account of his religious practices while in London. Unlike Woodforde, Lonsdale does not seem particularly interested in food and hardly ever mentions what he eats. That he was a country man is very clear. He hates the bustle of London and gives no indication that he enjoys the city in any way. From many references in his letters, he shows his keen interest in farming activities. Besides the land he farmed himself, it appears from the Crigglestone Land Tax returns of 1787 that he had a number of tenant farms, e.g. that of Samuel Kemp who is mentioned in the Letters. In the Crigglestone Township and Enclosure survey and valuation of 1800 Lonsdale's total valuation amounted to £83.11.6d.

The letters to his wife and those to the Revenue Office are complementary to each other. In his letters to his wife Lonsdale appears to be surprised and indignant that there are other dangerous claimants for the new lease. In the letters to the Surveyor General's Office a fuller picture emerges. In 1799 Lonsdale was aged 62, he did not live near Sunk Island and Margaret Gylby who had been the lessee for nearly 50 years, had done little in the way of embanking and improvements. It is not surprising therefore that during the years energetic and younger men had cast envious eyes on the island and realized its possibilities. All the claimants mentioned in the letters lived in the vicinity of Hull or Sunk Island and would appear to the Crown officials likely to undertake the various works and improvements more efficiently than an elderly clergyman living some miles away. Nor does Alexander Johnson, Lonsdale's legal adviser, emerge as a forceful figure and the Crown Officials imputation of delay seems justified to some extent. Lonsdale admits that Johnson postponed his arranged visit to the Island in September (Letter XII, pp. 64-5) because of his own family affairs in the country and actually did not visit the Island till November. However, in the years following the granting of the warrant in 1799, work on Sunk Island was extensive and continuous and Lonsdale himself was constantly there and one letter is written from the island itself. A list, dated 22 September, 1804 and therefore later than the last of the letters, of occupants of cottages on Sunk Island includes the name of John Lonsdale. The delay by the Crown in actually granting the new lease occasioned these letters written between 1800-1804 which give us such a detailed account of the various activities concerning the Island.

When in 1790 Elizabeth Lonsdale inherited a share of Sunk Island the Lonsdales received rents of £1,200 a year. When the new lease was granted in 1804 they appear to have received between £4,000 and £5,000 as their half share of the net rent.

John Lonsdale died at Newmillerdam and was buried at Darfield on July 13, 1807. At the time of his death his elder son, Jack of the letters, was in his first year at King's College, Cambridge where he had a distinguished career. Henry was still at school at Wakefield. His daughter Mary died in 1810.

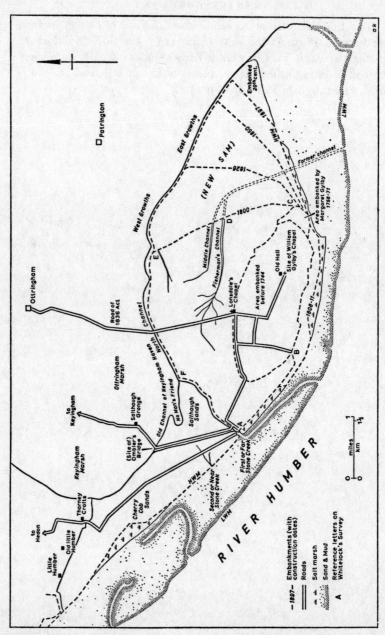

The stages of reclamation of Sunk Island

III. SUNK ISLAND

Sunk Island is an area of reclaimed land on the northern side of the lower part of the Humber estuary. Though originally an island completely surrounded by water, it is no longer so, for successive reclamations have joined it to the mainland; those undertaken by Lonsdale and his partner at the beginning of the nineteenth century as part of their agreement with the Crown agents made an important contribution to this development.

These reclamations were possible because of natural accretion here. Before the middle of the seventeenth century, however, loss of existing land rather than accretion of new land appears to have been taking place in the Humber. It is clear from the chronicle of Meaux Abbey that before the late thirteenth century there lay along the north shore of the Humber a broad strip of lowland with several villages or hamlets. During the later thirteenth century and fourteenth century, this lowland was progressively overwhelmed by tidal inundation. The *Meaux Chronicle* records storm surges and overtopped banks, ruined crops and vain attempts to stem the advancing water by new banks thrown up further inland.[1]

What remained of these low-lying areas was still in danger in the mid-sixteenth century. Exchequer commissioners certifying to the Lord Treasurer on "the State of Saltay", i.e. Saltaugh, a former monastic grange at this time held by the Crown, reported that in December 1554 there were "iij great breks" burst through the embankment by a recent storm and that a new "sea dike" further inland was necessary.[2]

Many stretches of this northern bank were suffering erosion from the effects of strong tidal scour, and jetties were built out into the river to deflect the streams from the shore. The 1554 certi-

---

[1] *Chronica monasterii de Melsa* (3 vols. Rolls Series 43, 1866-8) ii 300, iii 102-3, 182-5, 243, 283-6; J. R. Boyle, *The lost towns of the Humber* (1889), 73-6, 78-81, 88-91.

[2] P.R.O. E107/469/7.

ficate mentions "a Jetie which is made for good purpose for the
breke of the course of the Humber and putting of the stream from
shore", and several such jetties are marked on the earliest extant
chart of the Humber.

This chart, a hand-drawn sheet of paper added to an atlas of
proof copies of Saxton's county maps which once belonged to Lord
Burghley,[3] has been dated to about 1560.[4] It conveniently portrays
an important stage in the physical evolution of the lower Humber
because, by this date, the most serious losses had taken place, and
the memory of these lost lands may be preserved and the site of
future reclamation is indicated by a shoal marked on the chart and
labelled "quicke sande sene/called Sonke sande"; this is the earliest
known occurrence of the name. It is described as "sene" in contrast to others marked "unsene" presumably because it was visible
at low water whereas they remained submerged, a characteristic
which it retained for another century.

"As for its origins", an account written in 1719[5] states, "several
old people here can remember when there appeared nothing of it
but a waste and barren sand, and that only at low water, when for
the space of a few hours it showed its head and then was buried
again till the next tide's retreat: thus it continued until the year
1666, when it begain to maintain its ground against the attack of
the waves."

This change of condition which made reclamation possible after
the losses of earlier periods may be related to changes of sea level.
There are indications that in East Anglia sea level fell from a
relatively high position in Romano-British times, had come down to
a height similar to that of today by the third century A.D., and,
continuing to fall, introduced a period in which it remained depressed below present levels and which lasted until the thirteenth
century. Sea level apparently reached its lowest, about 13 feet below
present sea level in East Norfolk, about 1200 and then began to
rise again. This rise became more rapid after 1280 or 1290 and continued so until the seventeenth century after which, though the

[3] British Museum Royal MS 18 DIII ff62-3.
[4] G. de Boer and R. A. Skelton, The earliest English chart with soundings.
Imago Mundi XXIII (1969), 9-16.
[5] J. Chamberlayne, An account of the Sunk Island in the River Humber some
years since recovered from the sea, *Philosophical Trans. Roy. Soc.* London XXX
(1719) 1014; Abridged Trans 6,423.

tendency to rise persisted, the rate of rise decreased.[6]

Although there is little direct evidence from the Humber area[7]
such changes, if they extended here (and changes of sea-level can
hardly be local affairs), would, it seems likely, have made possible
an earlier settlement of these lowlands by the Humber, when sea
level was below its present height, followed by their inundation
during the subsequent rise. The slowing down of the rate of rise
in the seventeenth century might have allowed the effects of deposition of silt or warp in the estuary to become more obvious, for
shoals to grow to a condition where they were uncovered at low
tide and where reclamation began to be a possibility.

Such possibilities appeared in due course in several places in the
Humber, and reclamation work was begun at Sunk Island, Cherry
Cob Sands, Read's Island, and Broomfleet Island from the mid-
seventeenth to the late nineteenth centuries. This sequence of reclamations, generally progressively later in date the farther upstream
they lie, may be a consequence of the derivation of the Humber
warp or silt from the materials which coastal erosion washes into
the sea from the cliffs of Holderness and which the flood tide
brings into the estuary. This, though much discussed, appears to be
the likeliest source.[8]

Artificial reclamation could only be undertaken profitably after
a lengthy process of natural accretion. "The process takes place
principally in shoal water where the tidal currents are never strong.
Till the level of half tide is passed, the deposition of sediment is
probably slow, and can only take place at high tide when the water

[6] C. Green. East Anglian coast-line levels since Roman times, *Antiquity*, 35
(1961) 21-8; but for a discussion of the difficulties of such interpretations see A.
V. Akeroyd, Archaeological and historical evidence for subsidence in southern
Britain, *Phil. Trans. Roy. Soc.* Lond., A 272 (1927) 151-69.

[7] Recent excavations in Scale Lane, Hull, have revealed evidence of house rebuilding at the beginning of the fourteenth century. "The remarkable feature of
this rebuilding was the physical raising of the ground level of the house and yard
area achieved by the deposition of clay over the first dwelling which effected a
one foot rise in the land surface. This phenomenon has been noted in other excavations in the High Street area in Hull and indicates, I believe, a conscious effort
by the townspeople to raise the level of the settled area to a safe platform above
sea level which is thought to have undergone a significant change towards the
end of the thirteenth century." P. Armstrong, Field Archaeologist, Hull Museums,
Archaeological Excavations in Scale Lane, Hull. A preliminary report. December,
1974. Privately circulated.

[8] H. C. Versey, The Humber warp, *Proc. Leeds philosophical and lit. society*
(*Science Section*), 3 (1939), 553-6.

is still. Afterwards the growth of salt marsh plants binds the mud, and by straining out and entangling the particles of sediment, lengthens the time during which mud can be deposited. The marsh thus rapidly rises to within a foot or two of ordinary high water mark, and the growth gradually changes from samphire to sea-lavender, sea-blite and sea-purslane, then to thin wiry grass and afterwards to be flooded by the sea.

". . . when the surface is thus covered with vegetation, the land may at once be embanked, but if it is enclosed from the tide before it obtains a green carpet, it may be twenty years before it is of much value for agriculture, for scarcely anything will grow upon it."[9]

Naturally, not every part of a shoal reaches the same stage of growth at the same time; the parts where accretion is most rapid will be the first to pass through all the stages and, by attaining a cover of "better grass", to indicate their readiness for embankment. They will be surrounded by outmarshes, less advanced in the process, and their various degrees of advancement will be shown by the roughly zonal arrangement of the several communities of salt-marsh plants, each colonizing an environment which, in the length, depth and frequency of its tidal submergences, will be appropriate to its conditions of growth. These outmarshes will be intersected by an elaborate system of natural channels and creeks by which the water which covers them at high tide drains away during the ebb.

Accretion takes place where tidal streams are weak, and this may be near the shore, or between channels farther out in the estuary. It is possible to distinguish in a broad sense between channels in which the ebb stream is dominant and those where the flood current is stronger.[10] There is a tendency for deposition to occur between such channels, and especially near the heads of flood channels and the shore. Deposition in fact in all these conditions did occur on and near the site of Sunk Island and thereby engendered some conflicting claims of ownership.

The situation was straightforward in relation to Sunk Island itself. The ownership of the bed of the sea and of tidal rivers and

[9] C. Reid, *The geology of Holderness and the adjoining parts of Yorkshire and Lincolnshire* (Memoir of the Geological Survey 1885) 108.
[10] A. H. W. Robinson, The use of the sea bed drifter in coastal studies with particular reference to the Humber, *Zeitschrift für Geomorphologie*, Supplementband 7 (1968), 1-23.

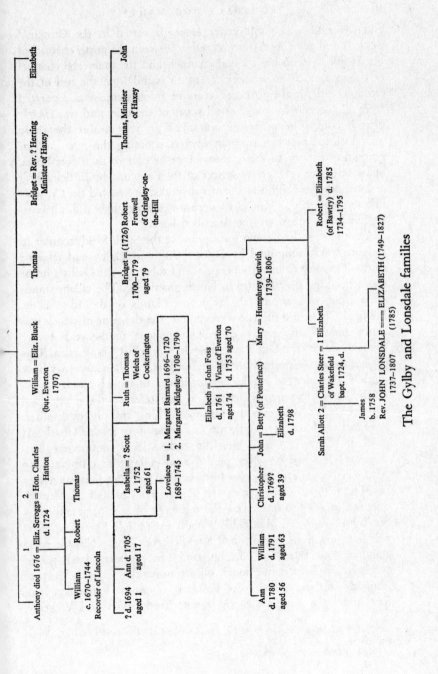

The Gylby and Lonsdale families

estuaries into which salt water enters is vested in the Crown.[11] Sunk Island developed from accretion between the north channel of the Humber, probably a flood channel, and the main ebb channel of the estuary. It arose therefore as an island from the bed of the estuary, and for the first 130 years of its existence was separated from Holderness by water at all states of the tide, and was clearly Crown land. The ownership of other growths nearer the shore was disputed between riparian owners claiming the new land as gradual accretions to their frontage, or as part of their foreshores, or by actual or prospective lessees of the Crown, who in defending or asserting their rights as tenants defended or asserted the Crown's title to ownership. Those of these disputes which have a direct bearing on Sunk Island will be described later.

A petition to the Crown for a grant of the Sunk Sand in order to reclaim it was submitted by Colonel Anthony Gylby and referred to the Treasury Commissioners on 8 October 1667.[12] Gylby's home was at Everton near Bawtry in Nottinghamshire. The village stands on a ridge overlooking the wide carr lands of the Idle valley, Hatfield Chase and the Isle of Axholme, the drainage of which was being undertaken, with royal encouragement, in the years before the civil war by the Dutch engineer Sir Cornelius Vermuyden. This experience of the possibilities of drainage and reclamation may have made Gylby alert to similar opportunities in the Humber.

The lease subsequently granted to him refers to the many good and faithful services done by him to the king and his royal father. A family tradition that Gylby on one occasion concealed Charles II in a tub of meal from Cromwell's soldiers lacks confirmatory evidence. Gylby had however played a prominent part in the long tenure of Newark as a royalist fortress from late 1642 to its surrender in May 1646 on orders from the King. The nucleus of Newark garrison appears to have been the regiment of foot commanded by Sir John Digby of Mansfield Woodhouse, High Sheriff of Nottinghamshire in 1642, who had attended the King when the royal standard was raised at Nottingham. The regiment later passed to Gylby, its lieutenant-colonel, who commanded it and a troop of horse during the last siege of Newark as one of four colonels of foot under the governor of the town, Lord Belasyse of Worlaby,

---

[11] Stuart A. Moore, *A history of the foreshore and the law relating thereto*, Stuart and Haynes, London, 1888.

[12] Calendar State Papers (Domestic) 1667, p. 516.

Lincolnshire. Gylby was one of those who signed the Articles of Surrender when the town submitted on the King's orders. He was out again for the King in the second civil war in 1648 and compounded for his estates in 1650. His involvement in the Nottinghamshire part of the abortive rising of 1655 led to his examination at Newark, the report of which describes him as "a dangerous enemy", and to his imprisonment at Nottingham.

Belasyse said of his officers at Newark that the nation had not better men than those he commanded in this siege of Newark, and when he was made Governor of Hull (1661-1673) after the Restoration, he was able to employ several of his veteran officers in the garrison there.[13] Their number included Gylby who became lieutenant commander of the fort and deputy governor. He and Andrew Marvell were elected Members of Parliament for Hull in 1661.[14]

Gylby's petition for a lease of Sunk Island stressed the newness of the land and its freedom from any competing claims of ownership—"to which Island no man hath any title nor has it been profitable to any nor ever yet any Beast or Sheep upon it, it being overflown every spring tide".[15] A description of the island in Gylby's time records the stages by which it became reclaimable— "at first a great bank of sand ... thereat other mud and matter stopt, and then still more and more by degrees.... The island when it was given to Col. A.G. was never quite overflown but at spring tides. At neap tides ... it was constantly dry and had on the highest parts thereof grass".[16] The Treasury referred the petition to the Surveyor General, Sir Charles Harbord, from whom Gylby "had an order to the Trinity House, Hull, and some gentlemen in Yorkshire and Lincolnshire to certify the condition of it".[17] In due course, the Surveyor General was able to report that an

---

[13] *Newark on Trent The Civil War Siege Works*, Royal Commission on Historical Monuments (England). London: HMSO, 1964, 56-7, 77; John Thurloe, *State Papers*, 7 vols., T. Woodward, London, 1742, iv, 484, 496; Alfred C. Wood, *Nottinghamshire in the Civil War*, Oxford, Clarendon Press 1937, pp. 147, 167.

[14] K. J. Allison, *A history of Yorkshire, East Riding, I, the city of Kingston upon Hull* (Victoria County History, Oxford, 1969), 113.

[15] Draft Report of Surveyor General to the Treasury, 22 February 1799 PRO CRES/2/1446. No confirmation has been found for Allen's statement (T. L. Allen, *A new and complete history of the County of York* (6 vols., Hinton, London, (1831), iv, 311) that the island first appeared in the reign of Charles I.

[16] *Leland's Itinerary*, publ. T. Hearne, 3rd ed., J. Fletcher, Oxford 1769-70, vols. Letter from Rev. F. Brokesby, 6 May 1711, vi, 107 (and n.), 108.

[17] Calendar State Papers (Domestic) 21 June, 4 July, 1668.

area four miles by one mile was capable of being embanked, but that he could not judge how much it would be worth when embanked, "finding it very barren, bearing only a salt broken grass with many bare places ... and there being no fresh water for the relief of Inhabitants or Cattle". He estimated the cost of embankments and sluices at £4,200, the maintenance of which together with jetties against erosion would be more than the land so reclaimed might be worth, and recommended that Gylby should be offered on such terms as would encourage him to adventure on this difficult project.[18]

The activities of rival petitioners had given Gylby some anxiety,[19] but these were allayed when on 19 June 1669, he was granted a lease for 31 years from Michaelmas 1668 at an annual rent of £5 which became due only after the first 100 acres had been embanked; the lease was to become void aften ten years in respect of whatever land remained unembanked.[18]

Seven years later, when only about 20 acres had been embanked, Gylby submitted a second petition, that because of the heavy expenses of reclamation, the terms of his present lease were a discouragement. To raise the money for the improvements he would have to sell the small estate he had,[20] which he was unwilling to do, and this would be largely for the benefit of the next lessee. Instead of the grant in perpetuity for which he asked, however, he was given, on 28 October 1675, a new lease for 99 years from Michaelmas 1675 at the same annual rent of £5.[21]

His efforts to reclaim Sunk Island involved him in charges of dishonesty. In 1663, the north blockhouse at Hull, part of the fortifications added to the town by Henry VIII in 1542, had been found to be ruinous, and Belasyse had been ordered to pull part

---

[18] Surveyor General's draft report, 22 Feb 1799 P.R.O. CRES/2/1446.

[19] Calendar State Papers (Domestic) 21 June, 4 July, 1668.

[20] "(The Corporation of Newark) have a manor in Harwell (near Everton, Nottinghamshire), which was Wentworth's heretofore I suppose. Thomas Magnus bought it and gave it to Anthony Gylby who was Lieut.Col. to Sr John Digby in Newark garrison, and, as I take it, is now tenant." *Thoroton's History of Nottinghamshire*, republ. with large additions by John Throsby, 3 vols. 1797, iii, 332. Gylby's will refers to "a certain messuage or tenement in Everton ... with a Carr called Everton Carr and a Close called the Haye alias Tintholme, now divided into several closes called Everton pastures ... all which I have in lease for three lives from the Right Reverend The Archbishop of Yorke." At the present time there is a Pasture Farm on Everton Carr between the village and the River Idle.

[21] Hull University MS DRA 527.

of it down and sell the materials to pay for the repair of the remainder. As late as 1681 the Ordnance office was investigating charges that he and Gylby had misappropriated the materials, the latter to build a house at Everton and another at Sunk Island. One witness, Joseph Osborne, a master gunner, wrote to the Ordnance Office on 17 February 1680 that on 4 May 1671, Gylby had commanded him "to take as much brick out of the North Blockhouse as would build a little house upon his land (called the Sunck)", and that bricks had been sent by water to Sunk Island. Belasyse was in Tangier for most of the time in question, and the accusation was directed mainly at Gylby, who professed himself unable to discover the papers recording his part in the transactions and feared that they had been lost when a ship carrying a trunk with his papers had gone down. The Ordnance Office informed Gylby that they would require him alone to account for or refund whatever had gone astray. The final outcome is not known. In a letter written from Everton 15 August 1681, he says he is too ill to proceed to London[22] and, indeed, he died in 1682.[23]

Despite the second lease, no very considerable progress had been made in embankment. The extent of his achievement is recorded on Greenvile Collins' chart of the Humber, which, though not published until 1693,[24] appears to have been made in 1683 or 1684.[25] It is the first chart to mark Sunk Island, rather than Sunk Sand; the embanked portion appears as a small polygon enclosing at most one eighth of the island.

By his will Gylby left his lease of Sunk Island and all his estate and interest there in trust for whichever of his three grandsons by his eldest son, Anthony, a London lawyer who had died in 1676,[26] first attained his majority.[27] Thus the eldest of the three, William, duly came into his inheritance

[22] J. J. Sheahan, *History of Hull*, 2nd ed. 1866, 338-44.

[23] Probate of his will was granted 20 July 1682, *Wills in the York Registry 1681-1688*, Yorks Archaeological Society Record Series 89, p. 25.

[24] G. Collins, *Great Britain's Coasting Pilot*.

[25] Hull Trinity House Fifth Order Book, 13 September 1683, records a decision to give Collins assistance in his survey.

[26] Calendar State Papers (Domestic) 23 June 1676. He was admitted a member of Gray's Inn 25 November 1658, married Elizabeth Scroggs, daughter of Sir William Scroggs, a Lord Chief Justice, and is buried in St. Andrew's, Holborn. His widow later married the Hon. Charles Hatton, younger son of Christopher, Lord Hatton of Kirby. She died in 1725 and is buried in Lincoln Cathedral.

[27] Will of Anthony Gylby, 10 April 1682, Nottinghamshire County Record Office.

of the island in about 1690. William Gylby, a lawyer of Gray's Inn and recorder of Lincoln from 1721, remained lessee for over 50 years and laid out a considerable portion of the handsome fortune he had made as a barrister on improvements, embankments, and defences against flooding.[28] "I have all along been and shall still continue to be laying out money in improving that place" he said in his will.[29] As early as 1693 he had raised £450 by mortgage[30] and in his will refers to another mortgage of £1,000, an encumbrance which however he paid off before his death.[31] His tenure of Sunk Island was indeed a vigorous one. The island was divided into farms, several houses and cottages were built, together with a chapel, Gylby himself paying a clergyman to take services there.[32] An undated petition of Gylby's asks the Archbishop of York "by subscribing one line or this paper, to signify only that he shall not be displeased if any of the Clergy in Holderness shall celebrate Divine Service". As the chapel was not consecrated, the clergy were unwilling to come without leave from the Archbishop. The Archbishop replied that as it was not certain whether the island was in Lincolnshire or Yorkshire, he could not interfere one way or the other.[33] At this time the island was about two miles south of Holderness and four miles north of Lincolnshire.

It is to William Gylby's period of management that Brokesby's description of the island in 1711[34] applies—"There are near 2,000 acres[35] inclosed with high banks to keep out the sea, which otherwise would overflow the island at high spring tide. Besides this, there are 6 or 700 acres more of a very good ground and of as fine grass as any in England, not inclosed, and therefore frequently overflown at high tides, on which they feed a great many horses and sheep. But though it be overflown, the water rises not much above the ground, so that it is soon dry again. Most of these horses and sheep are bred upon the island, and thrive very well, especially

[28] Surveyor General's Draft Report 22 February 1799 P.R.O. CRES/2/1446.
[29] Will 27 June 1737, letters of administration 28 May 1744. Borthwick Institute of Historical Research, York.
[30] Hull University MS DRA 528.
[31] Third Codicil to Will 28 July 1743.
[32] Whitelock's survey, see pp. 147-8.
[33] Borthwick Institute of Historical Research, York, Bishopthorpe Papers.
[34] *Leland's Itinerary*, publ. T. Hearne, 3rd Ed. J. Fletcher, Oxford 1769-70, vi, 107-8.
[35] In fact 1,560 acres, see below.

the horses which are chiefly of the large size for coaches.

"They have lately put several thousand couples of black rabbits upon it, whose furs are more valuable than the common grey.[36] The island has frequently been almost over-run with rats; for which reason they were forced to buy in a great many cats, to destroy them.... The present proprietor of the island has dressed these rats for food, but could never persuade his workmen to feed on them, though they might have had plenty for nothing.

"Some years ago they made a decoy upon the island which is plentifully stored with wild fowl especially ducks and teal. But it turns to little account for want of trees, which will not grow well here, by reason (as it is thought) the ground is too salt.... There are three houses upon the island, and eight men to take care of the banks and other matters."

Chamberlayne's account of the island in 1719[37] also stresses the quality of the crops and animals produced on it—"this island, which is of a very fact and fertile soil, affords good grass, corn, and hay, and is replenished with numerous flocks of sheep which are of larger size and finer wool than those in Holderness ... It is stored with vast numbers of rabbits which seem innumerable; their skins are counted the finest in England and are of a dark mouse, shagged and soft as silk." The income Gylby gained from Sunk Island was about £800 per annum.

The embankments were several times breached, however, and the great part of the inland inundated, especially in 1722 and 1735, causing such heavy losses and expenses that Gylby is said to have declared a few years before his death that he had never received any advantages from the island but was money out of pocket. At the time of his death in 1744 the area enclosed was 1,560 acres.[38]

He bequeathed the island to his cousin Captain Lovelace Gylby of Beverley, son of his father's younger brother William. This Colonel William Gylby, the William Gylby the elder of Everton of the mortgage of 1693 and second son of Anthony the first lessee, was, like his father, lieutenant-governor of the fort of Hull, and

---

[36] For an account of the importance of rabbits in the East Riding, see A. Harris, The Rabbit Warrens of East Yorkshire in the eighteenth and nineteenth centuries, *Yorkshire Archaeological Journal*, 42 (1967-70), 429-43.

[37] Chamberlayne, *op. cit.*

[38] Surveyor General's Draft Report 22 February 1799. Gylby was buried in Lincoln cathedral, 10 May 1744. Harleian Society 40 (1896) 1227-9.

also deputy-lieutenant of Nottinghamshire.[39] He was buried at Everton in 1707. Lovelace is described as a man of literary tastes and pursuits.[40] Family tradition asserts of him that he lost the lease in a drinking bout, and in any case he possessed the island only briefly for he died 11 September 1745 aged 56.

He died intestate and the lease passed to his widow, Margaret (née Midgley). She lived until 1790, and her long possession of the island was marked by several developments which were to be of considerable importance later, especially the two renewals of the lease granted to her, and the effects of continuing accretion to the shores of Sunk Island and to the adjacent parts of the north side of the Humber.

She first applied for a renewal of the lease in 1755 when it still had about 20 years to run. A survey of the island was accordingly made for the Surveyor General by William Burrows. It shows that there were 1,551 acres of dry ground, exclusive of many broad creeks and ditches, within the present banks which themselves contained 2,100 roods. The area reclaimed seems to have suffered some contraction as a result of the floods in William Gylby's time, for Burrows notes that there were another 1,173 roods of older banking outside the existing banks which had enclosed about 1,660 acres. An inscription on his map records four houses and a chapel.[41] The island was now reckoned to be worth £726 a year.[42] The new lease extended what was left of the existing 99 year lease, due to expire in 1774, to a term of 31 years[43] running from 15 March 1756 to 1787, an additional 12 years. The lessee, who entered into covenants to embank and enclose, was granted the island, estimated to have a total area, including outmarshes, of 3,500 acres, for a single payment

---

[39] Calendar State Papers (Domestic) 12 June 1698; 9 December 1700; 13 July, 12 September, 1702. Memorial to Lovelace Gylby, St. Mary's church, Beverley.

[40] *Famillae Minorum Gentium*, ed. J. W. Clay, Harleian Society, 40 (1896) 1227-9. The pedigree here and in Lincolnshire Pedigrees G-O. Harleian Society 51 (1903) 402 is confused by a failure to distinguish the two Williams, uncle and nephew, and assigns the latter, who in fact never married, his uncle's wife, Elizabeth Bluck.

[41] University of Hull MS DRA 529.

[42] Surveyor General's Report 22 February 1799.

[43] By the Act of Parliament 1 Anne cap.7 (1702) leases of crown land were not to exceed a term of 31 years. This was to check the alienation of crown lands which had gone on freely in the previous reigns. The Civil List was instituted in 1698 whereby, in exchange for a guaranteed income to the Crown, tthe Treasury received customs and excise duties and rents of Crown lands. The Treasury became concerned therefore to ensure that the source of part of its revenues was not dissipated and its income improved.

or fine of £1,050 and an annual rent of £5.[44] Presumably her intention in gaining the new lease was to secure to herself the maximum
advantage from any reclamation she undertook.

Some embanking was accomplished in the following years, for
a second lease, which was granted to her in 1771,[45] refers to 1,583
acres 2 roods 17 perches taken in before 1756 and 76 acres 1 rood
23 perches since taken in and encompassed with a bank at the
east end of the island.[46]

Natural accretion was also proceeding steadily on neighbouring
foreshores to the north and west of the island. The most notable of
these areas of accretion was at Cherry Cobb Sand, alongside the
north bank of the Humber immediately up stream of Sunk Island.
Here, as at Sunk Island itself, a shoal had reached the condition of
readiness for reclamation. It lay, however, so near the edge of the
estuary that it was debatable whether it was an island arising from
the bed of the estuary and separated from the shore by a navigable
channel now silted up and therefore crown land, or whether it
was an accretion on the foreshore and partly against the frontage
of the manor of Little Humber and therefore passed to a private
landowner. The Constable family of Burton Constable in Holderness, who had long maintained a claim to the foreshores of the
Seigniory of Holderness, and who were also lords of the major of
Little Humber, took the latter view, and asserted their ownership
of the new land, letting it for grazing.

In 1741 Roger Hall of the Hull Trinity House offered to take a
lease of the area from Cuthbert Constable, and when this was
refused petitioned the Crown for a lease so that he might embank
and reclaim, offering payment and to defend the Crown's title to
the land. Hall did not pursue his claim, nor did Joseph Thompson
who presented a similar petition to the Crown in 1748.[47] Then in
March 1759 a further petition was submitted by the Corporation
of the Sons of the Clergy, a charitable body founded in 1655 and
granted a charter in 1678 which bought land and applied the

[44] University of Hull MS DRA 530.
[45] University of Hull MS DRA 532. See below p. 2.
[46] This seems to be the "new intack" of Whitelock's survey (Plan reference
numbers 1 and part of 2). It is called the New Close in Richard Iveson's map of
1829 and John Bower's survey of 1830 (below, p. 37). The areas however do not
correspond exactly, and Bower's survey refers specifically to 67 acres 0 roods 21
perches added to the island by embankment about 1771.
[47] This account is based on University of Hull MSS DHO/14 and DDCC/22.

revenues to the relief of widows and orphans of deceased clergymen. The Corporation had become owners of Saltaugh Grange near to Little Humber, and the new accretion extended along the Humber foreshore from Little Humber to their own property; their application was for a lease of the 500 acres which adjoined their frontage.

William Constable, who had succeeded to the Constable estates on the death of his father, Cuthbert, in 1747, maintained the family claim to accretions on the foreshore against the Attorney-General, who in reply to the petition of the Sons of the Clergy had reported in 1760 that "Mr. Constable hath not an atom of title", that the right of the Crown ought to be asserted by an action at law, and that the petitioners ought to be encouraged by an offer of a grant on advantageous terms if they won their case. An information of intrusion was accordingly filed against Constable, and the issue came to trial at York Assizes in July 1763.

The Crown endeavoured to establish its case by showing that Cherry Cob Sand was an island grown up from the navigable bed of the Humber. They called boatmen as witnesses to testify that they had regularly sailed in keels carrying corn and other goods from Patrington Haven to Hull through the north channel between Cherry Cobb Sands and Holderness, and that they had seen Constable's men fixing stakes and faggots of thorn and furze so as to cause the channel to warp up. Constable countered by bringing evidence to show that the faggots were laid to check erosion rather than to promote accretion, that Cherry Cobb Sand was not an island because witnesses had been able to walk to it at any stage of the tide, and that the sailing marks used by the boatmen giving evidence for the Crown showed that they were using the channel to the south of Cherry Cobb Sand, not that to the north. Cherry Cobb Sand was different from Sunk Island to which Constable's ancestors had never advanced any claim.

The court's decision was for Constable, but the Sons of the Clergy were unwilling to accept this as a final conclusion and asked the Attorney-General to reopen proceedings by filing a fresh information against Constable. The Treasury refused to sanction further litigation at the Crown's expense but the Sons of the Clergy were again offered by the Crown a lease of Cherry Cobb Sand at advantageous terms if they were successful in a new action. The Attorney-General filed a new information against Constable in 1764, but the doubtfulness of the issue and the heavy costs they would face if they

lost made them ready to accept the terms proposed to them by
Constable the following December, a compromise that would resolve
the deadlock to their mutual advantage if not to the Crown's. If
the Sons of the Clergy at their own expense would secure a stay
of proceedings, he would lease them 400 acres of Cherry Cobb Sand
in perpetuity at a nominal rent, provided that the Crown would
abandon its claim also. Despite the reluctance of the Lords of the
Treasury, the substance of Constable's proposals was eventually
embodied in an Act of Parliament in 1766.

These events affected conditions on Sunk Island in a number of
ways. Even before embankment, the accretions at the eastern end
of Cherry Cobb Sand approached the growths attaching themselves
to the western end of Sunk Island quite closely. Futhermore this
spreading of mudflat and salt marsh must have greatly reduced
tidal flow in the channel north of Sunk Island and caused silting
here. The consequent replacement of open water by stretches of
salt marsh, mud flat and creek made access to the island more
difficult and definition of its boundaries more uncertain and led
to negotiations between Margaret Gylby and Constable on these
matters soon after he won the trial at York.

Silting in the initially wide channel between Sunk Island and
Holderness had gone on so as to produce extensive areas of out-
growth attached to each shore[48] and a central shoal divided from
these littoral fringes by a channel on each side. In due course these
various features acquired names which, in order from the Holderness shore to Sunk Island, were Ottringham and Patrington
Growths, the North Channel, the Newsam[49] (i.e. the central shoal)
the Fisherman's Channel, and the Inner Newsam or Sunk Growths
attached to Sunk Island. The North Channel carried mainly the
land water draining south from Holderness whereas the Fisherman's Channel drained the ebbing tide from the new salt marshes
of the Inner Newsam or Sunk Growths. To begin with, access to
the island had been by boat, but the new accretions made that no
longer possible. "The first road to the Island by land, and that
within Memory was from the Holderness shore at Ottringham
Marsh when the tides were out over the large Tract and at first

[48] The accretions on the Holderness shore were helped by the jetties put up as
defences against erosion. Whitelock's plan shows similar jetties at the east end of
Sunk Island.
[49] Probably a corruption of new sand.

the going down as it were into the Landwater Channel (now the North Channel) was very dirty, the Bottom firm, with a current of water in the summer time ankle deep and sometimes nothing, the further side dirty, then a plain sand to Fisherman's Channel, this considerably deeper and worse to pass than the former, and then sand to the bank of the island. Grounds were farmed at Ottringham Marsh by island people to open them a road to the river side or satisfaction made to those whose grounds they went over, but the increase of the warp increased for some time the depth in those channels and rendered the passage that way in the course of a few years very difficult and at length impassable."[50]

Margaret Gylby's lawyer was her brother Jonathan Midgley, a Beverley attorney;[51] his description of his client perhaps helps to explain her dealings with Sunk Island in general, not merely those with Constable. Her disposition, he said, "to live in peace and friendship with all her neighbours is well known ... and as she seems very easy and indifferent about extending her worldly possessions, so she is very ready to make any concessions that can reasonably be expected from her in order that the boundary between Sunk Island and Cherry Cobb Sand may be amicably adjusted".[52] The boundary suggested was the Stone Creek, but at this time there were two Stone Creeks. They are shown on Charles Tate's plan of 1760[53] as the First (or Far) Stone Creek nearer Sunk Island and the Second (or Near) Stone Creek nearer to Cherry Cobb Sand. The area between was substantial and there was some argument before Margaret Gylby agreed to concede the ground west of the First or Far Stone Creek to Constable on condition that he would agree to a road from Salthaugh to the island at a modest consideration. A provision that there should be a road to Sunk Island by Thorney Croft at a rent of 20 shillings per annum until the Governors of the Sons of the Clergy should be able to make a bridge or passage from Salthaugh over Keyingham Haven was accordingly added to the Cherry Cobb Sand Bill, which soon after completed its passage through Parliament. It was this road which later occasioned differences between one of the tenants of Saltaugh

[50] State of case of Henry Maister as Lord of the Manor of Patrington in respect of his claim of Newsam Sands, c.1787, University of Hull MS DDCC/71/10.
[51] Mayor of Beverley 1752, 1766, 1774 and builder of what survives as one of the most notable Georgian houses in Beverley, Norwood House.
[52] University of Hull MS DDCC/22/32, cf. Lonsdale's remark Letter II, p. 47.
[53] University of Hull MS DRA 531.

Grange, the Ombler who built the Ombler's bridge shown on some of the plans, and the Sunk Island lessees.[54]

The embanking of the new land was put in hand soon after Constable obtained his Cherry Cobb Sand Act,[55] and was completed by 1770 or 1771. The engineer employed in this was James Pinkerton,[56] later to be one of Lonsdale's rival applicants for the lease of Sunk Island.[57]

Constable's reclamation of Cherry Cobb Sand may well have prompted Margaret Gylby to contemplate further embanking at Sunk Island. Midgley wrote to Constable on her behalf on 2 March 1770 suggesting that as embanking of Cherry Cobb Sand was to begin shortly, the bank along the boundary with Sunk Island should be a joint undertaking rather than two individual banks. Constable replied that he saw no advantage in such an arrangement and that he would rather have his own bank to avoid occasions of dispute.[58]

It may also have been the possibility of further reclamation at Sunk Island that induced Margaret Gylby to seek at this time a renewal of her lease which had about another 16 or 17 years to run. It would clearly be desirable that she should secure possession of the island to herself for as long as possible in order to gain the full advantage of any capital expenditure on banks and sluices. She was granted on 9 August 1771 a new lease for a full term of 31 years, which extended her tenure for another 15 years beyond the term of her current lease in 1787.[59] For it she paid a fine of £1,550, an additional £15 annual rent until the expiry of her existing lease in 1787, and an annual payment of £100 thereafter. It was the approaching expiry of this new lease in 1802 which was the occasion of John Lonsdale's letters.

The survey taken when the new lease was taken showed that the rack rent of the estate would be £900, that it could be improved to £1,046, and that there were over 400 acres of outmarsh ready to be reclaimed,[60] a task which she professed herself willing to

---

[54] Letters XLVIII, XLXIX, LV. An alternative route was not available until a turnpike was made from Ottringham in 1841.

[55] 6 George III C. 66.

[56] University of Hull MSS DDCC/22/60-69.

[57] See letters VIII, IX, XI-XV.

[58] University of Hull MS DDCC/22/66.

[59] University of Hull MS DRA 532.

[60] Joseph Dickinson's plan of Sunk Island of 1783 (University of Hull MS DRA 534) shows 2,248 acres 1 rood 8 perches of ground "already fit to embank".

undertake without delay.[61] In fact she made no reclamation, a circumstance which attracted comment during Lonsdale's negotiations later and for which Lonsdale felt obliged to offer some explanation.[62] She may have been partly discouraged by Constable's rejection of her proposal for a joint bank.

Conditions on the north side of the island also were beginning to demand attention, and definition of the boundary there was necessary before any considerable reclamation could be undertaken, and her success in this provided Lonsdale with a useful argument to set against the lack of progress in embanking.[63] The description of the crossing from Holderness to Sunk Island quoted above stresses that, of the two channels between the island and Holderness, the Fisherman's Channel, which lay nearer to Sunk Island was the deeper, at any rate to begin with, and it was therefore the contention of Henry Maister, lord of the manor of Patrington, and Sir Christopher Sykes, an owner of land in Ottringham, that it was the proper natural boundary, and the large shoal called the Newsam between the two channels covering about 3,500 acres was therefore an accretion to their estates. The Landwater Channel or North Channel had become the deeper partly because the Keyingham drainage act of 1772[64] required that the water discharged from the sluice built at the island in the North Channel called No Man's Friend was to be directed down the lower part of the North Channel. This it was alleged had checked the natural tendency of this channel to warp up, whereas the island people had first put bridges across the Fisherman's Channel, and later placed dams and staunches in the western or upper part of it causing this channel, by contrast, to warp up smooth and level with the rest of the shoal. Having gained access by these means they had turned out large numbers of sheep to graze on the Newsam which had grown high enough for grass to grow. It was still possible for sheep to be brought from Holderness and there had been friction between the shepherds of the two flocks.

The problem was resolved in 1785 when Margaret Gylby brought an action of trespass against Sir Christopher Sykes and Henry Maister in the names of her tenants Stubbings and Roper. Two

[61] Survey of Sunk Island by William Ride Senior, March 1771, P.R.O. CRES/39/60, Surveyor General's draft report 22 February 1799, P.R.O. CRES/2/1446.
[62] Letter II.
[63] Letters I and II.
[64] 12 George III C. 64.

things seem to have told strongly for her. First, a view of the ground taken at her application showed that the North Channel was an open watercourse, whereas the Fisherman's Channel was partly warped up. Second, evidence was given that a ship had sailed round the island.[65] Though Margaret Gylby gained the verdict,[66] the lawyer's statement of the case for Sykes and Maister of about 1787 on which this account is partly based suggests than an appeal was contemplated, a circumstance which may well have deterred her from embanking the area while there was any chance that the verdict might be overturned. In any case she was by this time about 77 years old.

A valuation of Sunk Island was made by James Littlewood and Joseph Dickinson[67] in the year of her death, 1790, gives a total of 1,553 acres of enclosed land worth £1,649.17.6d. and 3,139 acres of "sands" worth £482.19.0d., in all 4,692 acres worth £2132.16.6d. Margaret Gylby died childless, and by her will left her interest in Sunk Island to be equally divided among the descendants of three of her husband's sisters, Bridget Fretwell, Elizabeth Foss, and Ruth Welch, all deceased. Several of their immediate issue were dead also so that the immediate effect of the will was to cause a considerable division of the responsibility for its management. Any vigorous action was improbable in such a situation. Moreover the lease had run more than half its term, and when, immediately after Margaret Gylby's death, the lessees applied for a renewal, they received answer that Parliament was at that time reviewing the management and letting of crown estates.[68]

A commission had been appointed in 1790 and the Act for the better management of the land revenue of the Crown (34 George

---

[65] University of Hull MS DDCC/71/10. It is presumably this incident to which Sheahan (History of Hull, 2nd ed. 1866, p. 730) makes an apparently confused reference in saying that Sir Samuel Standidge (a noted Hull shipowner who played a large part in developing the Greenland fisheries, and who in 1795 was both Mayor of Hull and Warden of the Trinity House, and also owner of land affected by the Keyingham Drainage Act), by giving evidence at the trial that he had sailed round the island to escape from a privateer in the Humber, had lost the island to the Constables. His evidence in fact lost Sykes and Maister the Newsam, and presumably the Constables also the area as part of the Holderness foreshores. According to one of their lawyers, the Constables never made any claim to Sunk Island itself (DDCC/22/25).

[66] According to Sir Edward Knatchbull (see below, p. 40) the case cost her £6,000, according to Lonsdale (Letter I) "above £500".

[67] University of Hull MS DRA 537

[68] Letter II.

III *C.* 75) of 1794 which implemented their recommendations modified the granting of leases in ways which directly affected the Sunk Island lessees. The maximum term of 31 years for other than building land was confirmed, leases were not to be renewed until within five years of expiry, and not before the making of a survey and an estimate of the improved annual rent. The crown was to receive an annual rent; the taking of an initial payment or fine was discontinued. Not surprisingly, little or nothing positive was done at Sunk Island; there was in fact some retrogression. Whitelock's survey describes some disrepair and neglect, including the cessation of the visits of clergy and the taking down in 1791 or 2 of the chapel which had become ruinous.

The lessees resumed their application on 31 October 1796 when their lawyer, Joseph Marris of Bawtry, wrote to William Harrison, the Surveyor General's deputy at the Land Revenue Office, to ask advice on how to proceed.[69] The summary of the events which followed contained in Lonsdale's letter of 12 March 1799 (XII p. 63) requires only slight amplification here. Harrison advised the lessees to submit a petition to the Treasury, and Marris in replying set out a statement of how the lease was held at present. Bridget Fretwell's third had been equally divided between her son Robert and her daughter Elizabeth, wife of Charles Steer. She was dead and her share passed to her own daughter, Elizabeth Steer, and John Lonsdale became possessed of this sixth part by virtue of his marriage to her in 1785. Robert Fretwell had died childless in 1795 and had left his sixth part to the lawyer Alexander Johnson in trust until a son of Elizabeth Lonsdale's should reach 21.

The children of Elizabeth Foss, William and his sisters, the recipients of another third part had all died by this time, and three-quarters of the third had gone to Elizabeth Foss, the unmarried daughter of John Foss, and the remaining quarter, or one twelfth of the whole, to Humphrey Outwith, widower of Mary Foss, a deceased sister of William Foss. Outwith later became Lonsdale's most active co-lessee.

Three descendants of Ruth Welch had shared equally her third share, and of these Ruth Horton, widow, and Farmery Epworth and his wife Elizabeth were still living, but of the remaining part,

---

[69] This letter and most of the other letters and papers of the Land Revenue Office concerning this application and referred to in this introduction or in the footnotes to the letters are in P.R.O. CRES/2/1446.

one ninth of the whole, six descendants of William Welch each held one eighth (one seventy-second part of the whole) and one married couple two-eighths.

It is not surprising that Harrison, faced with such a multitude of lessees, suggested that any new lease should be in the names of two of the lessees in trust for the others. A petition in the name of Alexander Johnson and others was left by Johnson in person at the Treasury in February, 1797. In acknowledging this to Marris, Harrison wrote, somewhat ironically in relation to what followed, "This business will unavoidably occupy a considerable space of time, probably several months, but your personal attention in town will not be necessary at any stage of it".

William Whitelock's survey was duly commissioned, made in the summer, and submitted in January 1798, and Marris, in asking in March for the terms on which a lease might be offered, reported that one of the lessees, Miss Foss of Pontefract entitled to three-twelfths of the estate and "in whose name jointly with Lonsdale the lease was proposed to be granted is lately dead, having made her will and bequeathed to her mother Betty Foss of Pontefract, widow, all her right and interest in the estate".

The outlines of a proposal for a renewal of the lease delivered to Johnson on 5 May 1798 set out that Whitelock had valued the 1561 embanked acres at £1,619.5s. per annum, the 3,208 acres outside the embankments at £316.4s. per annum, but improvable by the extent of £1,754, by a scheme of embankment and drainage estimated to cost £8,490, to a value of £2,070.19s., or the whole estate of £3,790.4s. gross[70] or £3,441.14.8d. clear. As the annual value of the whole island at present was £1,935.9s., the Surveyor General concluded that, making allowance for repairs to buildings and jetties and the rebuilding of the chapel, the rent for the first year of the lease should be £471.15s. and for the remainder £1,63815s., the lease to run for 31 years from 25 March 1798 or for 27 years from the expiry of the current lease. This however applied to the island as it then was; he would not feel justified in recommending a lease of the embanked part of the island to anyone who would not undertake to embank the outmarshes within a reasonable time. If the present lessees would engage to complete the embankments within the remainder of the present lease or in the early stages of a new lease, he would recommend that this

[70] There is an error in addition here; the figure should be £3,690.4s.

new lease should be granted to them, and as an encouragement he would propose that they should be paid their expenses out of the rents reserved to the crown. Before any specific terms could be proposed however, he required to know whether they would engage to do this, and how soon, and whether they could advance sufficient money for the undertaking and wait to be repaid from the rents due from the new land after it had been embanked, or from the whole estate by which they would recoup their expenses with less delay.

The Surveyor General had probably been made aware of the extent of the opportunity for reclamation by a report on drainage in south Holderness by Joseph Hodskinson, an engineer who had been engaged by Edward Constable to examine and report on the drainage of his property there. Hodskinson, whose report[71] was printed in 1796, sent copies to the Surveyor General, who, in April 1797, forwarded them to Whitelock and to Marris. Hodskinson's report proposed a comprehensive scheme of reclamation which would join Sunk Island to Holderness. Whitelock's first inclination was to agree but he later suggested the alternative scheme put forward in his own report. Whereas Hodskinson's scheme would have involved the co-operation of other land owners, Whitelock's avoided this complication and could be pursued independently by the lessees of Sunk Island.[72]

Lonsdale's letter describes how the lessees asked for clarification of some issues affecting the commencement of the new lease and the date at which the new rents would become due. The lessees had doubts also about the scheme of embankment proposed by Whitelock and preferred to do it by stages, and consulted other engineers and surveyors on the matter. Whitelock, however, when asked by the Surveyor General, maintained his first opinion of the preferability of having one ring of embankment rather than several smaller intakes. In answer to the lessees' query as to how long they might have the area to be embanked rent-free the Surveyor General calculated that they ought to pay a full rent on the newly embanked land of about £1,700, corresponding to the enhancement of its value, after eight years of the new lease, i.e. from March 1810, which would make the rent for the whole about £3,300.

All this took some time during which the apparent inactivity

[71] University of Hull MS DDCC/22/69.
[72] P.R.O. CRES/2/1441.

of the lessees encouraged other petitioners to apply. A Mr. Moody of Gringley, Nottinghamshire, a neighbouring village to Everton and home of Bridget Fretwell, Margaret Midgley's sister-in-law, had already asked to be allowed to negotiate if the present lessees declined. The application which most incensed Lonsdale, was that of James Pinkerton of Wombwell near Barnsley in association with his brother Francis from near Wakefield and John Leedham of Hull. They asked for a lease of the unembanked land in case the lessees were not renewing. As James Pinkerton had asked to be employed as the lessees' engineer and had learnt their plans, Lonsdale regarded this as such invidious double dealing as to justify an attempt to blacken Pinkerton's character.

The Pinkerton application increased the lessees' worries in one other important respect. Hitherto they had hoped that the Surveyor General would propose terms for the renewal. Now because the Pinkertons had made a specific offer, he felt obliged to ask the lessees to make him an offer. This unwelcome turn was embodied in a letter of 24 November from Harrison to Marris, telling him that the Surveyor General was ready to proceed with the renewal of the base, that "no unreasonable diligence would be required to complete the sluices of the whole ring of embankment by Michael-mas, that the interior works might be completed within the winter and summer following provided that the lessees found no difficulty in supplying the money that would be requisite for the purpose and that the term of eight years reckoning from the time when the works were completed would be sufficient to afford the lessees an adequate compensation for the expense of carrying the scheme of embankment into execution ... the Surveyor General presumes that upon this further view of the practicability of the measure and the time within which the embankment may be perfected the lessees may be enabled to found a proposal of the terms upon which they would be willing to take a lease of the whole island."

Another letter requesting an answer was sent to Marris on 26 December; two days later Moody was invited to submit terms to the Surveyor General "as it is uncertain whether the present lessees will renew or not", and Pinkerton on the same day submitted an application for the whole island. It was not until January 1799 that Marris advised Harrison that his letter of 24 November had not been received. The copy of the missing letter supplied by Harrison caused Lonsdale the "infinite concern" which occasioned his first letter.

The progress of the negotiations from this point can be followed from the letters themselves and their footnotes. Except where another source is stated, they refer to documents in P.R.O. CRES/2/1446.

The letters written after the making out of the Treasury warrant for the granting of the lease and his return from London suggest that Lonsdale, after coming successfully through the doubts, anxieties and hindrances of the negotiations, joined with Outwith in the task of reclamation and improvement with energy and enthusiasm. One of the letters is written from Sunk Island, another from Hull, others record visits, and a list of cottages on Sunk Island dated 22 September 1804 and sent by Jackson to Harrison[73] shows Lonsdale to be occupying one of them. The embanking of the outmarshes appears to have been completed by the early part of 1800,[74] and thus well within the period stipulated in the negotiations and laid down in the bond included in the lease.[75] As a result of this, by far the largest single addition made to its area, Sunk Island virtually ceased to be an island.

The lease,[76] however, was not finally made out until 12 December 1804, nine months after the last of the letters. By it, Sunk Island is demised to Lonsdale and Outwith in trust for themselves and the other lessees. Lonsdale's and Outwith's achievements are recited— the enclosing and embanking of 2,700 acres and upwards, the making of the necessary banks, sea walls, jetties, sluices, drains and the other works, the erecting of eight new farm houses and several other dwelling houses, cottages, outhouses and other buildings, and also a chapel,[77] costing in all upwards of £21,000. Of the total area of 9,432 acres 1 rood 18 perches, of which 4,389 acres 1 rood 13 perches are embanked, 2,729 acres 1 rood 13 perches were taken in between 1798 and 1801, the remainder being credited to Lonsdale's ancestors as in the 1771 lease.[78]

The lease is to run for 31 years from 5 April 1802, the inclusion of the extra three years asked for and granted in 1801[79] making

[73] P.R.O. CRES/2/1446.
[74] Letters XLIV and XLV.
[75] Letter XXXIV and n. 115.
[76] There is a copy of the lease in the University of Hull MS DRA 541.
[77] Sunk Island was made a parish and chapel its parish church by an Act of 1831 (II Geo. IV and I Wm. IV C. 59).
[78] Introduction, p. 27.
[79] Letter LII.

this new lease commence on the date of expiry of Margaret Gylby's second lease of 1771. The rent is to be £704.2.6d. for the first year, £2,090 for the second, and £3,190 thereafter. Various covenants, many of which are discussed in the letters, regulate the lessees' management of the estate, especially during the last five years of the lease. The lease was enterd at the Surveyor General's office on 6 February 1805 and enrolled by the Deputy Clerk of the Pipe on 28 February.

Neither of the principal lessees lived to enjoy for long their achievements in reclamation or the benefits of the lease. Outwith died 24 June 1806 and Lonsdale 10 July 1807. Lonsdale's will[80] divided the family's half share in Sunk Island between his two sons; John, the elder, when he came of age in 1809 was to have two-thirds, i.e. two-sixths of the whole island (one of which had been bequeathed to him by his great uncle Robert Fretwell,[81] see above, p. 30), and Henry Gylby Lonsdale, the younger son, was to have the remainder at his majority in 1812.

Further developments were put in hand, however, before the sons came of age. Notices appeared in the *Hull Advertiser* for 8 and 15 February 1808 inviting contracts for the making of two miles of sea embankment to enclose the outmarshes on the south side of the island, the work to be completed by Ladyday next. This enclosure amounted to 73 acres 3 roods 37 perches.[82] The Commissioners of the Ottringham Drainage in the same newspaper on 4 June 1808 advertised contracts to be let for the building of a bridge between Saltaugh and the island, the first indication of such a link with Holderness. A further 243 acres 3 roods 32 perches were embanked in 1811.[83] Accounts for 1818 and 1824 indicate that the lessees would receive about £6,193 and £5,861 clear of Crown rent for those years respectively.[84]

There was further accretion also on the north-east side of the island, and in February 1825 the lessees memorialized the Crown Estate Commissioners[85] expressing their wish to embank about

[80] University of Hull MS DRA 542
[81] University of Hull MS DRA 538.
[82] Bower's Survey, 1830 (see below p. 37).
[83] Bower's Survey, 1830.
[84] University of Hull MS DRA 543.
[85] An Act of Parliament of 1810 (50 George III cap. 65) passed the responsibility of administering the Crown estates from the Surveyor General to a board of commissioners. Except where other sources are specifically mentioned, the remainder of this account is based on materials in P.R.O. CRES/2/1441, 1444 and 1447.

1,200 acres here, but as there were only seven more years of the lease to run, insufficient for there to be a worthwhile return, asking for a renewal or extension of the lease. Their scheme was approved, but their application for a renewal or extension rejected. Instead the Commissioners agreed to pay one-third of the cost of the reclamation.

The work, which added 1,084 acres 2 roads 32 perches to the island,[86] was completed by early 1826, but because of the restrictive convenants in the lease, the lessees found it difficult to get tenants for the new land. These required that in the sixth year from the end of the lease they should sow grass over a sufficient area to reduce the proportion of tillage over the whole estate to not more than one half, proscribed during the last five years of the lease the growing of two white crops in succession, and also during these last five years required that at least half of the land in cultivation should be fallowed and the other half to be in clover ley after the cutting of one crop of clover from it. The lessees therefore petitioned the Commissioners 10 March 1826 for a dispensation from these conditions. The salt content of newly enclosed land needed a succession of white crops as the best means of bringing it into a proper state of cultivation either for tillage or grass. They set out their recommended system of cropping this;

1st Course	Year	Crop
	1826	(No crop) Ploughed and sown with Rape seed in June
	1827	Rape Seed
	1828	Wheat
	1829	Oats
	1830	Wheat
2nd Course	1831	— Fallow
	1832	Wheat
	1833	Oats
	1834	Beans
3rd Course	1835 etc.	— Fallow

It was eventually settled by articles of agreement in 1830 that for the remainder of the lease, they should leave unploughed the 400 acres of the 1826 enclosure which lay adjacent to the earlier enclosures and should till, manure, and fallow the remaining 680

[86] Bower's Survey, 1830.

acres "in a proper manner" that is, presumably, as required by the covenants of the lease.

From at least as early as 1813,[87] grasslands on Sunk Island and especially those of the 1800 reclamation had been ravaged by insect pests. The roots of grass and clover after about two years from sowing were so eaten by grubs that the land became bare, with scarcely a living plant on it. Rooks sought the grubs in such numbers it appeared as though pigs had been rooting up the ground. The lessees who, as early as 1816, had had consultations with William Stickney of Ridgemont in Holderness, one of a family widely known for their abilities as farmers,[88] favoured a treatment which they called the "Seeding System". This consisted of sowing grass or clover on fallow, allowing it to remain until it failed before the ravages of the grub, then ploughing and reseeding. If the land were left to itself to produce a natural grass, this would be poor and worthless, whereas by their system the land was kept in good heart, a succession of luxuriant crops of grass, white clover or trefoil produced, and far more livestock carried, and corn and straw grown than otherwise. Apparently this system had been followed since before 1820, but in the last years of the lease a dispensation from the covenants was required if it was to continue. The lessees petitioned for this 8 October 1829 and on 19 March 1830 the Commissioners were recommended by their surveyor, John Bower, to sanction the practice.

The last five years of the lease, the period in which applications for a new lease could be considered, began in April 1828. John Lonsdale had already applied on behalf of the lessees to begin treating for a new lease on 30 March 1827. The Commissioners had replied that they could not negotiate at that time, but had asked their surveyor, Bower, to value the estate. He had replied that the estate had been fairly managed and was in a proper condition. He had no recent plan of the estate but estimated the cultivable area at 5,800 acres and it annual value at £10,500. He was instructed to make a new survey. This survey, for which a map was made by Richard Iveson in 1829[89] was not completed and received by the

[87] Poulson, *History of Holderness* (T. Topping, Hull, and W. Pickering, London, 1841) ii, 465.
[88] P.R.O. CRES/2/1447. Poulson, *op. cit.*, ii, 369. A. Harris, *The Rural Landscape of the East Riding of Yorkshire 1700-1850*, University of Hull 1961, 125, 126-7.
[89] P.R.O. CRES/39/60.

commissioners until 4 January 1830, and in the meantime they had declined to open negotiations with any of the several applicants who had asked to treat with them for a new lease.

Bower remarked that the farm buildings were in some instances inadequate, that there had been few buildings before the granting of the current lease and that the large reclamations of 1800 had made new buildings necessary. The new buildings then put up at the lessees' own expense "were hastily erected ... of bricks and other materials, in some instances, not of good quality or well put together". He noted also that the tenants of Saltaugh were still refusing to accept rent from the lessees for the use of the road and recommended the making of a new road from the chapel to Ottringham.[90]

It seems that by the time Bower's survey was ready, the most important competitors were the existing lessees and their sub-tenants. These last had asked in January 1830 that they might become tenants of the Crown if the lessees did not wish to renew their lease, and in December, that their application might be preferred to that of the lessees. Their farms were less profitable than formerly but the lessees, despite falling prices and other difficulties, had demanded their full rents; if they or any other middle man were granted the lease, they, the sub-tenants, had little hope of being able to make a living on the Island.

The lessees, after some delay, submitted their own rather despondent application on 4 September 1831. They pointed out that the former Surveyor General, John Fordyce, had declared that their enclosures had been executed with a spirit of enterprise and liberality highly creditable to the lessees and beneficial to the estate, that the enclosure of 1825-26 had been unprofitable, that they had expended more than £30,000 since 1801, not one shilling of which had been repaid by the Crown except £1,137.10s., and this was less than the third part of the cost of the 1825 enclosure which they should have received. They were owed above £2,000 arrears of rent by their tenants. John Bower, in his survey, had calculated that these tenants might pay a total annual rent of £10,741. Deducting from this £411 for outgoings and five per cent, amounting to £516, as a reasonable profit to the lessees, left £9,814, and this,

---

[90] An Act (6-7 William IV, C. 91) for the making of a turnpike road along this alignment was passed in 1836. Poulson, *op. cit.* ii, 465.

it had been intimated to them by Lord Lowther,[91] would be the annual rent required by the Crown under a new lease. The lessees put the annual value at £8,005, reckoned outgoings at £700, a reasonable profit to themselves as £2,100, and £5,025 therefore as the appropriate rent to be reserved to the Crown. They doubted, so long as any rent near £9,000 was required, whether there was any intention on the part of the Commissioners to grant them a lease that was at all beneficial. "... But we cannot allow the renewal to be relinquished without an appeal to the justice of his Majesty's present Commissioners ... we now conclude by requesting a renewal lease of the Island and Outmarshes for 21 years ... at a reserved rent as near £5,000 as you will be pleased to grant it."

The lessees were probably near the mark in their belief that there was no intention to offer them acceptable terms. Bower had advised the Commissioners that the terms should make no allowance for the unprofitability of the 1825 reclamation; the lessees should accept the results of their bargain, gain or lose. Their assessment of a third part of the cost was based on a somewhat inflated assessment of that cost. The estate was in any case too large to be suitable for letting as one unit, and to absentee lessees.

The way was thus open for the sub-tenants on Sunk Island to make their own bargain with the Commissioners; as against Bower's valuation of £10,741, they offered £8,353, and finally obtained leases on their farms for rents totalling £9,140.10s. The acreage under cultivation was reckoned as 5,929 acres. The increase of 4,368 acres between this figure and Whitelock's total of 1,561 acres embanked indicates the extent of the lessees' achievement since 1799.

Francis Raynes in a report of 1 November 1830, presumably made after the rejection by the Commissioners of the lessees' offer, recommended the revision of the boundaries of the sub-tenancies so as to make proper sized farms. He also criticized the mode of reclamation followed in 1826. "A person well skilled in warping would have had the whole surface level ... at the present it is so full of small creeks as to prevent some parts from being converted into tillage ... The tide should be let in and a few cuts made to let off the water from the hollows when the tide recedes, as the whole must be perfectly dry ... In fact in the whole scheme of warping much depends upon laying the grass dry between

[91] M.P. for Westmorland and First Commissioner of Land Revenue.

tide and tide as otherwise the warp cannot be regularly deposited over the whole." He recommended that the tenants should be allowed more discretion in the management of their farms and expressly dissented from Bower's opinion in believing that the proportion of grassland advocated by the latter was unnecessarily high.

The Lonsdale's connection with Sunk Island concluded on a sourish note with a wrangle over the extent of their liability for repairs and dilapidations at the end of their lease. It was assessed at £931.5.4d. After allowances for repairs done by the outgoing lessees, the final transaction followed shortly after 22 September 1834 when Bower was instructed to issue a receipt for £755.19.4d. to the lessees, discharging them from any further liability.[92]

The harder bargaining of the Commissioners at the end of the lease no doubt reflects in part parliamentary criticism of their management of Crown estates. One such occasion was a debate in the Commons on 30 March 1830[93] in which the Commissioners were attacked by Mr. D. W. Harvey, M.P. for Colchester, for the easy terms of several leases including that of Sunk Island, whereby the lessees had been able to make excessive profits. The last audit, he declared, had shown that the lessees had received £9,600. The lessees of Sunk Island had been defended by Sir Edward Knatchbull, the member for Kent, who had referred to the "eminent services" of the lessees' ancestors to Charles II. A report of the debate in the outspoken newspaper *The Examiner*, celebrated for its attacks on the Prince Regent in 1812 and the consequent imprisonment of its proprietors John and Leigh Hunt, elicited from William Iveson, one of Lonsdale's rivals in 1799,[94] a comment on the leasing of Sunk Island in the form of a draft letter to the editor which, though not published, provides a suitable conclusion to this account of the Lonsdales' connection with the place.[95] "The Editor of *The Examiner* in his paper of the 4th inst.[96] has put

[92] P.R.O. CRES/2/1447.

[93] Hansards Parliamentary Debates N.S. (2nd Series), 23, 9 March–7 April 1830, col. 1055.

[94] Letters IX and XV.

[95] University of Hull MS DDCC/41/16. In defending Lonsdale and the Land Revenue Office and Treasury in this way, Iveson was perhaps not completely disinterested, for he was at this time trying to obtain a lease of Foulholme Sands which lie upstream of Cherry Cobb Sand and adjacent to "a small property" of his, Little Humber, which was occupied at that time by a son of his also called William.

[96] 4 April 1830.

forth some extracts from the speeches of Mr. Harvey relative to the Crown Lands and of Sir Edward Knatchbull in defence of the present lessees of Sunk Island and from the materials thus put together has drawn his remarks on the corruptions of ancient and modern times. The speech of the Hon. Member for Colchester as reported in the newspapers does not convey so clear an idea of the localities of Sunk Island as might have been expected from a man who had purposely visited and surveyed the Island, neither was the Hon. Bart. quite fortunate in his explanation of the means by which the present subsisting lease was obtained.

"Those who are acquainted with the history of Spurn and of Sunk Island know that the one is consequent upon the other. The first lease of Sunk Island was granted by Charles II as has been stated to Robert [sic] Gilby Esq., the date 1676 [sic] and the term 99 years. It was at that time overflowed by the spring tides and Mr. Gilby embanked about 30 acres. Whether the lease was granted in requital for services performed by Mr Gilby to the King or whether those services were more deserving of the pillory or halter or 30 acres of land we will leave to *The Examiner* to determine. The embankment thus made had the effect of stilling the flow of the tides and promoted the deposit of mud and additional embankments followed. About 20 years before the expiry of this lease viz in 1756, and in the reign of George II, this lease was surrendered and a new one granted for 31 years by the terms of which it does not appear that any reference was made to the services performed by Mr. Gilby to Charles II. Another surrender and renewal took place in 1771 and here be it remarked that the original lease granted in 1676 for 99 years would have continued until 1775.

"Next came the renewal which has been so much the subject of remark. The terms were agreed upon in 1800 or 1801 some short time before the expiration of the subsisting lease. The letting was not a job but was open to public competition. I was one of a party who delivered proposals at the land revenue office and if our terms had been higher than those of Mr. Lonsdale and his partners I have no doubt we should have obtained the lease notwithstanding any connexion between Robert Gilby Esq. and King Charles II. There were other companies who declared proposals as well as that in which I was engaged but I understood that the terms offered by Mr. Lonsdale were the highest and most advantageous for the Crown. The adventure turned out fortunate, there may be room for envy but I think none for any blame to any party.

"As a friend to fair play I trust you will during this recess give room in your columns for this letter. I shall follow the example of your correspondent on behalf of the Jews, give you my name and address, and sign myself

Your humble servant,
Submersus."

I

[*John Fordyce Esq.*[1]]

Newmillerdam Jan. 24- 1799
near Wakefield

Sir,

It is with infinite Concern I have been just informed, that a
letter written by your Direction to the lessees of Sunk Island was
never rec[eive]d, and consequently unanswer'd. The Circumstance
is a very extraordinary one, and of such a Nature as to determine me
upon presuming to assure You, that the most earnest Attention
has been paid to the Proposal you favoured us with, founded on
Mr Whitelock's Estimate.[2]

The Sum necessary to compleat the Works is indeed a very serious
one; but we have no Doubt of being able to advance it, and to
finish them in the time specified by Mr. Whitelock: reckoning
from this next Lady Day. We have at present a Number of Men
repairing the old Bank, w[ch] has been greatly injured by the late
Tides; and whom we intend employing in the new Embankment,
as soon as the Terms of the new Lease can be settled.

With Respect to these Terms we must throw Ourselves upon
the Clemency of Government, and cannot entertain a Doubt of
Justice being done us. As our Argument for such Clemency, You
will pardon me for reminding you, that Sunk Island was originally
granted by King Charles 2[d] to our Ancestor Col. Gylby[3] Gov[r] of
Hull for the Term of 99 Years, "in Reward", as is express'd in the
Grant, "of his faithful services", the King having promis'd under
his own Hand during his Exile to remember him, if ever He
returned to his Kingdom. The Embankments and Improvements

[1] The Surveyor General.

[2] William Whitelock, son of William Whitelock of Swinton in the parish of
Masham. Baptised October, 1745, in Masham church. He was employed by John
Fordyce, Surveyor General, to make a survey of Sunk Island. See Introduction p. 3
and Survey.

[3] Anthony Gylby, 6th son of Sir George Gylby of Stainton, Lincs. Married Ruth
daughter of Robert Rogers of Everton, Notts. Buried at Everton on April 27
1682. See Introduction pp. 16 *et sequens*.

have been all made by the Family; and I will only beg leave to add, that our Predecessor in the present Lease Mrs. Gylby[4] defended and secured fourteen Years ago at her own Charge in a Suit at York the Rights of the Crown to the Outmarshes, ag[ain]st the Lords of the Manor Sir Christ: Sykes[5] and Col: Maister[6] wch cost her above £500. And you cannot but suppose, that I am anxious to preserve to my Children an Interest in an Estate, thus obtained by their G^t. G^t. Grandfather.

We are told indeed, that there are a great many Applicants for these Lands; nay even, that there are some Persons, whom we have now consulted about the intended Embankment, basely attempting to procure them for themselves[7], But we have too high a Sense of your Honours and Judgement to fear for a Moment such Adventurers.

I sh[oul]d certainly have done myself the Honour of waiting upon you in Town at the First Opening of this Business, if I had not understood, that it was necessary for it to pass in a regular Process thro' the Offices; and more especially, as Mr. Johnson of the Temple,[8] who is a Trustee for my Son,[9] had kindly undertaken to transact it for us: But if you think my personal attendance necessary, and will give me Leave to [wait] upon you, I shall be always ready to obey your Order.

I hope Mr. Johnson has before this time presented our Memorial[10]

[4] Margaret, daughter of Jonathan Midgley of Beverley, a lawyer, who was mayor of Beverley in 1720 and died in 1746. Wife of Captain Lovelace Gylby 1689-1745, son of William Gylby and grandson of Anthony Gylby, first lessee of Sunk Island. After the death of Lovelace, Margaret became lessee. She died in 1790 and her memorial and that of her husband are in St. Mary's Church, Beverley. See Introduction pp. 22 and 28.

[5] Sir Christopher Sykes (1749-1801). An energetic Pittite M.P. for Beverley 1784, who obtained a baronetcy for his father, the Rev. Mark Sykes in 1783 and succeeded him at Sledmere, East Yorkshire, as second baronet the same year. He subsequently sold his Ottringham estates. He was the father of Mark (1771-1728), the famous bibliophile who possessed one of the best private libraries in England. See Introduction p. 28.

[6] Ibid.

[7] Introduction pp. 8, 33.

[8] Alexander Johnson, youngest son of Allan Johnson of Wakefield, solicitor of Wakefield. Admitted a member of the Middle Temple 1773, called to the Bar 1776, bencher of the Middle Temple 1812.

[9] Introduction pp. 6, 9, Letter III, n. 25.

[10] This memorial and petition (P.R.O. CRES/2/1446), undated but drawn up in December, 1798 (see Letter XII) in the names of all the lessees states that they were willing to accept the Surveyor General's proposals for a lease of the lands already embanked on the terms set out in Whitelock's survey, the new rents to

for establishing a new Lease; at least, he will do it in a few Days: And I shall be rendered most happy by hearing of its being bro[ugh]t to a good Conclusion. I beg of you, from the Necessity of the present lease, to pardon the liberty I have taken with you; and am with great Respect,

Sir,

Your most obed[ien]t humble Servant
J. Lonsdale.

II
[*to William Harrison*]

Newmillerdam
near Wakefield
2:^d Feb: -99-

Sir,

I have only been favoured with your letters[11] this Morning, owing I suppose to the great Fall of Snow upon the Roads. I sit down immediately to acknowledge the kindness of the Surveyor General in giving an Answer to my Letter to Him, and in excusing my

---

be payable from the expiry of the current lease, that they were also willing to follow Whitelock's plan for the embanking and draining of the outmarshes, and proposed to begin on Lady Day (25 March) next, but hoped that they would not be required to finish the work before the end of 1801, i.e. before the end of the current lease (Introduction p. 31, Letter XXVII, n. 102) and, because they would be doing this during wartime when money was scarce and labour dear on an island subject to inundation, they also hoped that they would be allowed the outmarshes rent free for at least 12 years from March 1802; eight years, suggested by the Surveyor General as the period during which they would not have to pay rent for the reclaimed land (Introduction p. 32), would hardly repay the outlay and the newly embanked land would be unproductive for three or four years.

[11] A letter of 28 January from Harrison, the Surveyor General's deputy, to Lonsdale, in which the Surveyor General reminds Lonsdale of the great length of time the lessees had held the island under three successive grants, the low terms on which it had been held and was still held, the vast advantage the family had had from it, "so great as to afford an ample compensation and reward to the family".

The Crown could complain that more of the island had not been improved by the family. There were thousands of acres of outmarsh which had long been fit for embankment, but there had been no new embankment for more than 50 years.

Several applications for the lease had been made by persons unknown to each other, all of whom had specified the rents they were willing to pay. The Solicitor

personal Attendance in London, wch however I had intended paying the beginning of next Week.

I am willing to hope, that the Surveyor General upon reconsidering this Subject will not adhere too rigidly to the Terms proposed in your letter. His Proposals, delivered to us last May along with the Whitelock's Report[12] were these, "If the Lessees are willing to compleat the Works proposed within the remaining Term of the present Lease, or in an early Stage of a new One, I will recommend to the Lords of the Treasury to grant a new Lease to them of the whole Estate". Now this we are entirely willing to do, and "to wait for the Return of our Money out of the Rents of the Lands to be embank'd", I therefore humbly hope, that the Surveyor General will have the Goodness "to state the Terms upon wch such Lease will be granted", and not continue to insist upon Ourselves offering Terms[13] wch are to be look'd upon as final, and might subject us from a trifling Difference to the cruel Hardship of losing our Lease.

I am sorry to find the Surveyor General thinks we have been guilty of unnecessary Delay in this Business, and wch I can truly assure him was entirely unintended, and arose principally from M^r: Johnson's continuing longer in the Country than was expected. It was always our Wish to have our Lease settled in time to begin the Works in Spring, and as we have three Years unexpired in our present Term both of the Old and New Lands, we thought there was time sufficient for finishing our Improvements. And it is I hope a sufficient proof of our Seriousness in this Matter, and we have been at a great Deal of Trouble and Expense in contriving and estimating the best Method of Embankment: And I can say with Truth, that our most accurate Calculations by no means fall short of those of the Whitelock's. The Buildings, I believe, are likely to rise much higher. With Respect to the Complaint, that

General had made it a rule not to communicate any of these terms to the other applicants. The result of these applications would altogether depend on the terms they offered. The present lessees having consulted engineers and valuers and having had Whitelock's report for 12 months ought to be able to make up their minds. Notwithstanding the other applications, the preference of renewal would be given to the present lessees provided their proposals were not lower than those of the other parties.

[12] Introduction p. 31.
[13] Introduction p. 33.

no more Land has been embank'd for so long a time, I beg Leave
to state, that Mrs Gylby the late Lessee held the Estate near 50
Years; and being only allied to the Family by Marriage did not
choose to expend more Money upon it for their future Benefit.
But immediately upon her Death, nine Years ago, the present
Lessees applied to the Government for a new Lease[14] thro' Mr.
Wilberforce,[15] who is a distant relation of M^{rs}: Lonsdale's[16]; And
the Answer receiv'd was that as the Crown Lands were then going
under the Consideration of Parliament, no new Lease c^d. be granted;
and we afterwards found, that 5 years before the Expiration of the
old Term was the time fixed upon. Under these Circumstances
and the Lessees having only just enter'd upon the Possession of
the Island, I think that the Surveyor General will not wonder at
their not embanking.

I sh^d be very uncandid not to own, that Col: Gylby's Family have
rec[eive]d an ample Reward: But yet I am sure, that it will not
be denied that some little Preference is still due to a Family, by
whom the original Embankment of the Island was made and without wch it is even probable the Land w^d not at this Day been known
to be the Property of the Crown.

But it is time to make an Apology for the Tediousness of this
Letter; and wch nothing but the extreme Importance of the Subject
can justify: For however inferior the future Advantages of Sunk
Island may be to me, yet they will be very essential to a Clergyman
with only small Preferment, and a Family entirely to educate.

I will now therefore repeat what I said in my former letter, that
I depend entirely upon the Justice and Clemency of the Surveyor
General, and am ready to enter into a new lease upon such Terms
as shall appear to him from M^r: Whitelock's Report to be fair and
reasonable; I say, I am ready to do this Myself as a principal Lessee;
even tho' the Rest sh^d. hesitate to join me in it. And I promise most
faithfully, that not a Moment's longer Delay shall be incurr'd. Be
pleased to present my serious Thanks to the Surveyor General for
the Favor contained in your second Letter, "that the Preference
of a Renewal shall be given to the Lessees": And I trust that the

[14] Introduction p. 29.

[15] William Wilberforce 1759-1833, M.P. for Hull 1780-1784, M.P. for Yorkshire
1784-1812, emancipator of slaves and friend of one of the rival applicants for the
lease of Sunk Island, a Mr. Thompson of Hull (Letter VI, and ns. 41; 42).

[16] His wife, Introduction p. 6.

same Goodness will indulge us with one single Letter more from you, stating the Terms upon wch such Lease will be granted.[17] I entreat you to lay this Letter immediately before the Surveyor General, and to believe me to remain most truly,

Sir

Your most oblig'd Serv[an]t

J: Lonsdale

III

Friday 4 o'clock

[15th Feb.]

My dear Betty[18]

Mr. Johnson brought me your letter yesterday and I rejoice to hear you are well. I hope you would receive one from me this morning. I had not time to add the Postscript or my Name to it, from the Letter Carrier[19] calling sooner than I expected. You will also have received the Surveyor General's Answer to my second letter and which you need not send to me, having seen a copy of it sent to Mr. Johnson, and also of my own to Mr. Harrison. You see how regular they are, and you will not be sorry to hear that Mr. Harrison says in his Note to Mr. Johnson, "Mr. Lonsdale's Letter is a very good one". I mention this because you are certainly entitled to the principal part of it. We have announced ourselves

---

[17] Harrison wrote to Lonsdale on 8 February in answer to this that the Surveyor General was not able to favour any one applicant by disclosing the terms offered by the others or the specific terms proposed by the Revenue Office, unless these were disclosed to all "which would lead to the disposal of the lease by public auction or something very like it which the present lessees probably would not wish to be adopted". The Surveyor General, if he felt able to make a proposal of terms, could not name any lower than those of the highest offer already received. The lessees had the materials on which to frame an offer. Harrison wrote to Marris on 9 February that "the Surveyor General is very impatient to receive the offer of the lessees".

[18] His wife.

[19] Letter carriers were employed by the Post Office. From 1792 they were supplied with uniforms. They were divided into three classes, those who carried the general post, those who carried the penny post which only operated in London and a few other large towns and those who carried foreign letters. Wages ranged from 11/- to 22/- a week. After 1767, houses were numbered and the letter carriers went from house to house. Until 1846 they rang a bell as they walked the street collecting letters. Those who carried letters for the General Post conveyed them to the General Post Office in Lombard Street where they were sorted. Mails were then dispatched at 8 p.m. and carried by the Mail Coaches.

as being in Town, in readiness to wait upon the Surveyor General whenever he may be pleased to call upon us. So that the present Interval is a very anxious one. I mean to myself for I only see Mr. Johnson and Marris at Dinner which we have by candlelight at half-past five o'clock.[20] I have sent a Note to Mr. Bolland[21] and Hardcastle[22] but was unwilling to be absent from my Post, until things are got into some kind of Train. You may depend upon my attending to every possible avenue to our success but I don't yet see the Propriety of applying to Mr. Wilberforce or Mr. Smythe.[23] We must just see what ground the Surveyor General shall take. If your own letter reached Bruton Street,[24] perhaps little more can be done. If you think otherwise, tell me in your Answer to this. Mr. Marris will have it, that the S.G. has some *particular* Person to serve, and means to deter us by his Terms. Our memorial was intended to obtain rather better terms than Mr. Whitelocks but I am determined to accede fully to his Estimate as being the only true Point of Defence. If this Post! is not tenable, we must then immediately go a little higher. I have a Notion myself things will even come to a Crisis and it is very well it should be so as I assure you our Plan is here a very expensive one. Mr. M. would not be satisfied without our having a Front Parlour and our Dinners are not of the most frugal kind. I will next pass on to poor Jack[25] for whose best Interest I never cease to feel. If you think from Mr. Sumner's[26] Letter that his morals are not in danger, Eton seems to be the

[20] Dinner was the chief meal of the day and a very big one. Earlier in the century two o'clock was the usual hour but by the end of the century a much later hour was favoured in polite society.

[21] John Bolland, 1742-1829, eldest son of John Bolland, shop keeper of Masham. He is buried at Fetcham, Surrey. Introduction p. 4.

[22] Probably a son of William Hardcastle, solicitor, of a well known Masham family, died 1782. Either Thomas b. 1750 or William, b. 1751.

[23] John Smythe 1748-1811 of Heath Hall near Pontefract, M.P. for Pontefract 1783-1807. Lord of the Admiralty 1791-1794. Lord Commissioner of the Treasury 1794-1802.

[24] Smythe's London residence.

[25] John Lonsdale 1788-1867, elder son of the letter writer. Born at Newmillerdam, baptized at Sandal Magna. Educated at Heath School and Eton. Admitted King's College, Cambridge, 1806. Ordained 1815 and married Sophia Bolland the same year. Chaplain to Archbishop Manners-Sutton, Principal of King's College, London, Archdeacon of Middlesex. Bishop of Lichfield from 1848 until his death. See *Dictionary of National Biography*.

[26] Robert Summer, son of the Rev. John Summer, headmaster of Eton. Scholar at King's from Eton 1767. M.A. 1774. Vicar of Stoneleigh and Kenilworth 1773-1802. Married Hannah, daughter of John Bird, alderman of London.

proper Place and quite as much so *without* the Island as *with* it. For he might then be the maker of his own Fortune. And if this point was once settled, the sooner he went to Mr. Rogers[27] the better: I mean if he will undertake to prepare him in the proper Books, for in *this* Respect you see Mr. Wilkinson[28] has declined taking him. Would there be any harm in your requesting your Brother to ask him this Question, and this immediately for the sake of having no more time. Till you write me again, let Jack be going through such Parts of Terence and the Greek Testament as he omitted reading at School before. My good opinion of his willingness to make sure ground encourages me to hope this from him. I forgot to mention in my last, that Mr. and Mrs. Mawe[29] were confined with us at Baldock. She of course speaks very highly of the great Care taken of Boys in her mother's House. Mr. Smith a Tutor boards in the House, and frequently comes to Mr. Stanhope's in the Summer and whose Son is lately gone there. We are just returned from the S.G. who has received us very politely. He promised to lay our terms before the Treasury and to give us a decisive Answer in a week or 10 Days[30] so that I really hope we shall obtain our Lease upon Mr. Whitelock's estimate. For upon that I openly avowed to the S.G. I had been long determined to stand or fall. Now, to poor Jack again. I think a public school is best, either Eton or Westminster. If Eton is preferred, the sooner he goes to Mr. Rogers the better. If Westminster, he may go again to Heath.[31] Mr. Bolland says Westminster is the Seat

[27] Thomas Rogers 1760-1832, headmaster of Wakefield Grammar School, 1795-1814. A famous preacher whose confirmation classes were so well attended by townspeople as well as candidates that an evening lectureship was founded in 1801 to which Mr. Rogers was appointed.

[28] Robert Wilkinson for fifty years was headmaster of Heath Grammar School where Jack was educated prior to Eton. In 1840 Jack composed an epitaph to his former headmaster and his wife which is in Halifax Church. Mrs. Wilkinson earned high praise as being a mother to the boys and it was during her time that the boarding side flourished.

[29] John Henry Mawe, prominent in Wakefield society. Governor of Wakefield Grammar School 1785-92.

[30] The Surveyor General's draft report to the Treasury is dated 22 February. A letter from Harrison to Thompson says that the Surveyor General intends to report to the Treasury 23 February. Other references to it in other documents indicate 1 March. See Letter VII.

[31] The Queen Elizabeth Free Grammar School, Heath, Halifax was founded and granted a charter in 1584. Under the headmastership of Robert Wilkinson the school became celebrated and many attended from a distance. Jack went to the school at the age of six and was there from 1794-99. The period of having

of Corruption. I think there is a chance of my getting home next week but go on in your Plan of giving Notice for Afternoon Duty only.

J.L.

IV

Friday 4 o'clock
[15 Feb.]

My dear Mrs. L.

I have just called for my Letter again to correct a mistake in it, but find it is gone to the Post Office but I think you will not grudge the additional Expense of this when you see my mistake came from my eagerness to come home again. I have said there is a chance of my getting away from this place next week; but it must, at the soonest, be the week after even if the S.G. keeps his Promise to us. And before that time I will write to you again. So that if I should be longer detained Mr. Armer's[32] Turn will come again. I am going tomorrow with Mr. B. to Clapham. I will call at the Booksellers the first vacant time. The man wants to lay the cloth and I must conclude myself with my warmest love to yourself and children, most affectionately yours

J. Lonsdale

New Hummums[33]

---

boarders was a short one and later the school deteriorated and did not attract scholars from a distance. Elizabeth Lonsdale's accounts include an entry "total expenses at Heath for 4½ years £244 or £54 a year average".

[32] John Armer, ordained 1771, assistant curate of Chapelthorpe 1775-86, curate of Darfield 1786-93.

[33] In 1681 Henry Harris leased buildings in Covent Garden in order to establish a "hummums or bagnio". Richard Lazenby, a surgeon who claimed to have knowledge of the methods used to construct rooms for sweating and bathing from observations at Aleppo in Turkey, designed baths at the rear of Harris's houses. These were completed by 1683 and proved very popular being among the earliest Turkish baths constructed in London. Hummums also provided good lodging for any person desiring to lodge there. The price for sweating and bathing was 5.6d., to lodge all night 10s. Hummums was destroyed by fire in 1769 together with many neighbouring houses. In 1769-1770 the area was rebuilt and a Thomas Harrison took over three houses which became known as New Hummums Coffee House or Tavern and Hotel, "an excellent place for bed and breakfast with the convenience of hot and cold baths".

V

My dear Betty

I have really scarce time to sit down to write to you. We were engaged most of the morning yesterday at the Revenue Office, and are going again To day with another Petition to the Surveyor General.[34] Notwithstanding all their Objections and Difficulties started, I am still of Opinion they cannot help granting us a new Lease upon Whitelock's Estimate. We make a Push to day for some further Indulgencies. I have written to Mr. Smythe to thank him for his polite Attention to your Application. I find it will be very uncertain when our Business can be completed. You must go on in getting the Chapel supplied as well as you can. With respect to the Fast Day,[35] if you hear nothing more from me on Saturday I think you had better let Geo. Dyson[36] give Notice for no Duty at the Chapel, which will give to the devout a Power of attending at Sandall or perhaps it might be better not to give any notice about it and to send on the Tuesday evening to such Persons as have a Right to expect such Attention, and to Caution Geo.D. not to ring the Bell and to inform his Neighbours. Take which of these methods shall appear most prudent to yourself. You need not engage for the Sunday following, till you hear from me again. I hope to be at home myself. If we succeed in getting our Lease, the works are to be begun immediately: therefore it may be necessary to return by Bawtry and to concert proper measures with Outwith[37] etc. And if that should happen to be the Case, I will give you a line to send Horses for me there. Pray remind Joe[38] to get all his work done. He requires two Horses: which will give opportunity of picking the black Horse and making him handsome for your summer use. I wish very much to hear what becomes of poor Jack. If we stick

[34] A copy of proposals from the lessees of 19 February accepts Whitelock's valuation but asks that the full rent be reduced to £3,000 per annum.
[35] Ash Wednesday.
[36] Verger at Chapelthorpe.
[37] Humphrey Outwith 1739-1806. Introduction p. 30.
[38] Employed by Lonsdale for work on the glebe and general maintenance.

to the Eton plan, and it seems perhaps the best we can adhere to, there is no time to be lost in preparing him for it. I feel strongly with you, that the shaking of the Yorkshire method of speaking is of great Consequence. The Time fixed for the Closing of the Application for the Island is Saturday next,[39] when we shall know our Fate. I know you think me too sanguine but I will venture to encourage you by even saying that we cannot lose our Lease on the ground we have taken. An Appeal would lay [sic] to the Lords of the Treasury. I wish only our Bargain may prove a good one. You may expect a final Letter on Monday or Tuesday next. I have nothing left of my cold but a little tickling cough which is nothing. The Fat Cow never came into my head till this moment. Send for Sam Kemp[40] and let her be kept or sold as he advises. Desire Jo. not to neglect the Sheep and to attend particularly to the corn threshed. If you saw the Bustle of our present situation you would forgive the incoherence of my letters. I pray every night for you and the children.

Yours faithfully,
J.L.

VI

Monday, [25 Feb.]

My dear Betty

I have received both your Letters and I am made happy by hearing you continue all well. As you seem to wish Jack may remain with you till my Return, you must absolutely insist upon his getting two Lessons in a Morning and two in the Afternoon in such parts of Terence and the Greek Testament as he had omitted at School. If he refuses doing this, assure him from me, that he shall spend the next Vacation at School for that Purpose. I mean, if possible, to follow your Advice of going to Eton and then coming to a final Determination. But you will say, tell me something about the Business in question. I wish it was in my Power to give you a good account of it. The Horizon has been blackening ever since my last

[39] i.e. 23 February.
[40] His name occurs in the Crigglestone land tax returns of 1787 and in the Enclosure Survey of 1800 when he appears to be a tenant of John Lonsdale. Crigglestone adjoins Chapelthorpe.

letter to you; fresh Applicants pouring in,[41] and Mr. Wilberforce himself making Interest for a person "to whom he owes the greatest obligations".[42] I have written to Long[43] and waited upon him. I have also called at Mr. Smythe's and left a card. The S.G. says Mr Pitt[44] will govern everything himself. I think still they cannot reject our Petition with any Regard to Character or Decency. God knows how it may end. My companions in this Business are eating, drinking and talking merrily "never thinking of the Flood that may overwhelm us". You will readily believe I don't myself sit in so easy a Chair. You may depend upon my Closest Attention. I have visited no body but Bolland. The oysters were never sent off and therefore I hope we may still enjoy them. I will now stop my Pen in hope of seeing Mr. Harrison who is invited to Dine with us To-day but will very probably not chose to talk upon the

[41] In addition to those already submitted by Moody and the Pinkertons and Leedhams (Introduction p. 33), the following further applications had been received:—
John Foster of Bewick in Holderness, Richard Terry of Hull merchant and Samuel Thornton, M.P. for Hull, 26 January; T. Thompson of Hull, 6 and 9 February; J. A. Worsop of Howden Place, Howden, Yorkshire, "having sundry estates near the Ouse and the Trent, which by great attention and expense he had protected from these rivers, and therefore well acquainted with the improvement of such lands," 23 February; A. Yeale for himself and Leedham, the Pinkertons having withdrawn, 23 February, and joined by a Mr. Wood, 24 February.

[42] Wilberforce had written to the Surveyor General on 29 January on behalf of Thompson. Thompson was born in Holderness in 1753. For some years he was a clerk with Wilberforce and Smith, Baltic merchants, who occupied Wilberforce House, Hull, Wilberforce's birth place. Wilberforce retired from the business in 1784, and a new company was formed, Smith and Thompson, bankers. Thompson was for a while M.P. for Midhurst, Surrey. He retired from business and public life in 1820 and wrote some works of local history especially *Ocellum Promontorium* (1821), *Ravenspurne* 1822, *History of Swine Church* 1824.

[43] Charles Long, 1761-1838. He entered Parliament in 1789 and was appointed joint secretary to the Treasury in 1791. He resigned with Pitt his patron in 1800, and on Pitt's return to power in 1804 was made a Lord Commissioner of the Treasury. He was created first Baron Farnborough in 1826. He was "a respectable official and a successful placeman", and a great friend of Pitt (*Dictionary of National Biography*).

[44] Pitt's concern for better management of the finances of the nation and his measures of reorganization including the Crown Lands Act of 1794 (Introduction pp. 29-30), are clearly reflected in the firm attitudes Lonsdale met in his negotiation, and especially in his encounters with the Treasury. During 1799 the Government was in great financial difficulty. The Budget (itself an introduction of Pitt's) of December 1798 showed an excess of supply over ordinary revenue of £23,000,000. Income tax was introduced for the first time and it is not surprising that the Government was anxious to obtain as much as possible from the lease of Sunk Island.

Subject. The Deception of their Civility is so great. I will in the meantime tell you a Circumstance which vexed me confoundly at the time, but which I hope you will only laugh at. The very second walk I had with Mr. Johnson to look at St. Paul's my Pocket Book was taken from me. I had hold of his Arm all the way, a Situation I find they often take Advantage of. It luckily contained no Bills, and may perhaps be of service to me. I shall in future take particular care of my watch etc.

Mr. Harrison came to us at half past five, so that I had no Power of closing this Letter last Night. I am sorry to add, that he now speaks very doubtfully of our Success. He goes so far as to recommend it to us to have an Advocate to defend our case before the Lords. The Memorial is not yet laid before them but expected to be in a few days.[45] Mr. Wilberforce's friend is a Mr. Thomson of Hull. Another principal Bidder is a Mr. Foster of Beverley or Hull connected with the Persons Mr. Jackson[46] mentioned to you having given up.[47] His plan is said to be that of occupying it himself, for which reason he may certainly afford to give more than ourselves. I am sure you will pity my unpleasant situation. Prepare for the worst that may happen. Would you venture to engage in the Lease with a Prospect only of clearing 500 L per Annum in the whole and which I think it would not fail to do at 20 s. per Acre? I shall be glad to hear from you by the Return of Post and tell me positively what you wish me to do. There is another question I must beg your answer to. If the Lease is not got, is it still your Intention to send Jack to Eton and do you wish me to go to Eton before my return. It is high time to have this Point absolutely decided and therefore let us try to act together for the best. My Mind is at present little fit for bold Decision. I explained the matter fully to Mr. Wilberforce by Letter. He was not to be seen when I called upon him. My application to him at Buxton had entirely escaped his Recollection. Can anything more be done? What did you say to Mr. Smythe. It would perhaps not be right to trouble him any more. If the S.G. leans to Mr. Wilberforce's Application for his Friend, all is over.

[45] The memorial was submitted to the Treasury on 1 March together with the Surveyor General's report and the other applications.

[46] An attorney of Hull acting for the lessees, who married Mary, second daughter of Humphrey Outwith. See Letter XLVII.

[47] The Surveyor General's list of applications (n. 45 above) shows that Terry and Thornton withdrew their application on 16 February, but that Foster had applied on his own behalf 19 February.

I cannot suspect the Lords to be against us.

Send for Mr. Armer and take care of everything as well as you can.

I will keep my Post as long as you wish me to do it.

Kiss my dear children for me.

Yours truly,

J.L

VII

Sat. [2nd March]

My dear Betty,

I thank you for your very good letter. We have been busy this morning in drawing up a Petition to the Lords of the Treasury. I think it will be so strong as to carry conviction to Mr. Pitt, "if Lord Carrington[48] has not hardened his Heart". But we find that they are most intimately connected. Mr. Harrison recommends it to us to make our Word to Lord C. He compares him to a Mole, bad to throw out of his Ground, I am also to present a Copy of our Petition to Mr. Wilberforce and Mr. Smythe to solicit their Assistance. Our Memorial is not even yet presented by the Surveyor General. He promised to do it last Saturday, or Monday and certainly on this Day. It is now to be postponed to next Thursday. The reason alleged is, that Mr. Fordyce wishes first to see Mr. Pitt and which is not very easy to do. I mention all this to show you how very uncertain my coming home is. Mr. Marris begins to grow impatient but I am determined to see the End, if it can be done in any reasonable time. I think there be no time and consequently no use in writing to Mr. Bird. I agree with you about making a Bargain, tho' the present Profits may be but small. But I keep this to myself; Mr. Marris and Mr. Johnson being of a contrary opinion. Some suggestion I find have been made against our

---

[48] Robert Smith, 1752-1838, M.P. for Nottingham from 1779 until 1797 when he was created first Baron Carrington as a reward for his fidelity and support of Pitt, of whom he was a close friend. He had several links with the southern part of the East Riding of Yorkshire. The Smiths, a banking family (Robert was a partner in the bank), were partners with Thompson, Lonsdale's rival applicant, in the Hull bank of Smith and Thompson (Letter VI, n. 42). In 1780 he married Anne, daughter of Lewyns Boldero Barnard of Cave Castle, a few miles west of Hull, and in 1802 he and his three brothers, George, Samuel, and John, became freemen of Hedon just east of Hull, with a view to George standing as parliamentary candidate, a process in which Iveson (see Letter IX, n. 56 and Introduction p. 40) would have been much involved.

want of Ability to undertake so large a Business. I shall insert in our Petition that we are willing to give all reasonable security. I admire your Fortitude in saying that a Failure in our Application will not give you a moment's Pain. You shall hear from me again, as soon as anything can be said to the Purpose.

I shall follow your advice in going to Eton the first two days I can command. I shall very probably be forced to stay all Night there. Let Jack then stay at home, till I write again which shall be immediately after. But by all means and without Delay answer Mr. Wilkinson's Letter in the handsomest manner you can. What is said against Rogers has very little weight with me. The less time he devotes to school, the more he would have to spare as a private Tutor. But if Dr. Heath[49] approves of it, he had better be sent up after the present Easter Vacation. Let me repeat to you again and again, keep him closely to his Books. If he goes to Eton *now*, it will be of the best consequence to him. With Respect to the Income Bill, make yourself Master of it, as well as you can and state any Difficulties which occur to you by the Return of Post. Mr. Hardcastle has called upon me several times; but I wish to keep myself entirely disengaged.

The weather is extremely warm and close here. Let Jo. stick to his Farming and get all his [work as] forward as he can; I mean consistently with your going out which I would not by any means prevent. In hopes of hearing a continued good account of you all.

I am yours
J. Lonsdale

VIII

[7 March]

Dr B.

I had determined not to write to you any more till I had been at Eton, and had fixed my going for tomorrow. I am very unpleasantly driven from my Purpose by a Necessity of attending the Revenue Office in the morning. We believe the Board have sat to-Day, and must use our best means to explore the Result. We have already heard, that James Pinkerton and his Brothers in Law

---

[49] Son of Benjamin Heath, book collector of Exeter. Scholar at Eton. M.A. 1771, D.D. Lambeth 1791. Master at Eton 1775-91. Headmaster 1792-1801. He died in the cloisters at Windsor in 1822.

have overbid us by 600 L p. ann.[50] If you can substantiate anything against his Character and Circumstances proper and worthy of being shown to the S.G. you must send it immediately. If you cannot you had better remain silent. He is a most daring fellow, having solicited the Treasury for more time to view the Island again and still advance in his Bidding.[51] If they submit to this, there is an End of all public Faith and Honour. I have had an Audience of Mr. Wilberforce; he promises not to oppose us. Mr. Thornton[52] has done the same. We have waited also on Lord Carrington who bluntly told us it will go the highest Bidder. I have just returned from Mark Lane where I have written to Mr. H. Thornton and sent it by Mr. Bolland. You may depend upon nothing being neglected. I mean with caution. Johnson swears he will file a Bill of Equity against them.[53] I shall continue to persist in all prudent

[50] The Pinkertons had withdrawn 23 February, but Yeale, with whom they had been associated, made an offer on behalf of himself and Leedham amounting to about £2,916 p.a. for 31 years for the whole island, compared with Pinkerton's earlier offer which corresponded to an annual rent of £2,562. Tht lessees' offer at this stage, calculated as an annual rent, came to £2,679, Moody's to £2,057, Foster's to £2,416 and Thompson's to £1,223.

[51] Yeale wrote to the Surveyor on 2 March that he "had no idea of such a sharp competition for Sunk Island" and asked for extra time in which to make a more accurate examination, and on 9 March asked for yet further time.

[52] Samuel Thornton of Clapham, Surrey. M.P. for Kingston upon Hull 1784-1806. Son of John Thornton, biggest merchant trading with Russia who made large contributions to Government loans. The family was involved in the evangelical movement and was connected by marriage with William Wilberforce and through him with Hull. Thornton consistently supported Pitt.

[53] Johnson's exasperation provoked him to write, 7 March, to Stubbing (see Letters IX, XV) ".... to my great surprise many proposals have been offered some by men of high character, who to their honour it should be spoken, when told the old lessees had had terms proposed to them withdrew their offers, some others not in such high situation but I presume from speculative motives have been induced to offer terms, and to their shame be it said are determined not to withdraw them, but as I can't class them with those before mentioned, their ignorance of honor and their selfish principles I presume is [sic] their guide to injustice. But I am more astonished than I can either write or describe at the sight of a letter from Hull this morning mentioning you to be associated with others endeavouring to obtain the lease from your present landlords ... nothing shall satisfy me that you can be guilty of such wicked conduct but the certificate of your guilt under your own hand.'' Thompson sent a copy of this letter to the Surveyor General offering to withdraw his application "if the present lessees have any just claim of preference and if I cannot fairly and honourably with regard to them make any offer for the estate". The Surveyor General replied on 16 March "I know of no right which any person has to say that the Crown may not like any other proprietor treat with other offerers nor which can render it more indelicate for any person to make an offer for one of the Crown's estates than for an estate belonging to an individual".

and temperate Means. If you love Jack, keep him rigidly to his Books. If you relax, he is ruined. I will write to you after I have been at Eton. God restore [me] to you and my children.

Yours affectionately,

J. Lonsdale

Thursday evening [7 March]

I wished you would send a Letter of Civility to Mrs. Deane, if you think it can be done with Propriety, Perhaps she has left the House. If you still think it proper to address a Note to her, perhaps you had better antedate it, mentioning my being absent from home. What makes me mention this exclusive of the Good manners of it, that she may have it in her Power to serve us.

P.S. What I mean by substantiating is, will the Persons deliver in writing what they have said, if found necessary?

IX

Sat. [March 9]

My dear Betty

You say you don't grudge Postage; and if you did, I should still continue to write to you, whenever I have half an Hour to spare, and anything to say likely to give you Pleasure, or Information. There was a Board Day at the Treasury yesterday, but alas nothing done, nor, we now learn, can be done, till Mr. Pitt himself attends; and which you are sensible is very uncertain. Mr. Marris therefore is resolved to return, and I hope you will readily believe I am eager to accompany him: we have for this Purpose waited this morning at the Revenue Office for Leave of Absence. Sorry am I to add, that my own Continuance for a week or two longer is recommended by Mr. Harrison: but which perhaps you will consider as no bad symptom. His words are these, (but really they are often "vain words") "Your Appearance and Character are respectable and your personal Application, as well as Letters have had great weight with the Surveyor General, and perhaps you may have Reason not to repent your having staid in Town a fortnight longer". If this Fortnight was all, you are sure I would bear it for the Love I bear my children, not to say yourself. But to come home to you at last without success would add greatly to my mortification. I will not however, as I promised you, quit my Post, till you join with me in opinion about it. Mr. Marris proposes returning on Tuesday. Col. Drummond,[54] who is now in Town, has with great good Nature spoke to Mr. Thornton in our Favor, but from his warmth against the Ministry rather overshot his mark. He says an imputation of Delay is brought against us. Mr. Harrison advises me to defend myself against this Charge in a Letter to the S.G.[55] I will embrace the opportunity of introducing Pinkerton's Treachery who is now considered as the most dangerous opponent: being determined, as I told you in my last, to bid most unreasonably. If you can bring any solid charge against him I would shew it to Mr. Harrison, but trifling hear-say Evidence would do no good to our cause. It is neither pleasant, nor creditable to be fond of criminating.

We have snow here and the air very damp and cold. My Breast is a little affected with it but I have followed your Prescription of L.Hill's Balsam. If the weather will permit, I will go to Eton on Monday or Tuesday and then write again. I fear you will be shocked when I tell you our own Tenant Stubbing is joined with Thomson and an Attorney in Hedon against us. I have written according to your hint to Ramsey to obtain a letter from Mrs Midgely.[56] You are right in supposing Miss Foss's shares to be given up.[57] It is with great Difficulty I screwed it out of Marris. What a Devil he is! With respect to Duty, tell Mr. Brown,[58] that Mr. Armer shall assist him on G. Friday: and if there be occasion for it, which God

[54] Colonel Hay Drummond of the 5th West Yorkshire Regiment, a brother of Lord Kinnoul. He lived not far from Lonsdale at Bawtry.

[55] See Letter XII.

[56] Stubbing is named as one of the tenants of Sunk Island in Dickinson's Survey of 1783 and in Whitelock's. He was one of the tenants in whose name Margaret Gylby established in 1785 that Sunk Island extended to the North Channel. The Hedon attorney was William Iveson, (1764-1843) eight times mayor of that place and under-steward to the Constable family. At this time Hedon had features of both a rotten and a pocket borough and elections were closely managed by Iveson and his brother James in the interests of Pitt's Tory party. See Letter XV. For an account of the Iveson family see M. T. Craven, *A New and Complete History of Hedon*, (1972) Chap. 10. John Ramsay, a lawyer, was mayor of Beverley in 1775 and 1792. Margaret Gylby left him a legacy of 100 guineas. Mrs Midgely was probably Jonathan Midgley's widow, (Introduction, p. 29). She also received 100 guineas.

[57] In fact Mrs. Foss. Miss Foss had died and bequeathed her share to her mother (Introduction p. 30). See Letters XXVII p. 90, XXIX p. 94, XXXI p. 99 XXXIII p. 102, XLIV p. 120, LVII p. 133, and n. 143.

[58] Rev. William Brown. Educated Clare Hall, Cambridge. B.A. 1760. M.A. 1763. Usher Wakefield Grammar School c. 1771-95 and governor 1809-1818. Instituted to Sandal Magna 1793, resigned in 1818.

forbid perhaps Mr. Wood[59] may assist on Easter S. or he may do for once without.

[There is no signature]

X

[March ?]

Dear Betty

Involved in the great Question of the Island, I have quite forgot to take Notice of another principal Point, poor Jack's going to School. I have been considering, that even on a supposition of his being removed to Eton after the approaching Easter Vacation it is a Pity he should remain idle all that time. What I would therefore recommend to you is that you should send him immediately to Mr. Rogers the moment you receive this Letter. Give my particular comp. to him and tell him I shall esteem it a particular Favor, if he will consent to take him, instructing him in the Eton G. Grammar,[60] writing Latin verses and in such Books as may best prepare him for Eton. You may send to him a short list of the Books used in the 4th Form. You will say perhaps, what good can he do in so short a time. I answer that it will at least prevent the dangerous effects of doing nothing. And indeed nothing can excuse me not mentioning this sooner, but the supreme and continued Agitation of Mind I have been under since I came here. What you say about my having had so much time for walking about has hitherto been ungrounded. If I continue longer, it is likely to be the case. I have not seen Mrs. Maw or any Person except Mrs. Thirkell[61] and Mr. Bolland.

The best method perhaps would be to get your Brother to intro-

[59] Rev. William Wood succeeded John Armer as curate at Chapelthorpe in 1784. In 1796 he was appointed a J.P. for the West Riding and lived at Woodthorpe House in Sandal. He died 1825 and was buried at Sandal.

[60] *Graecae Grammaticae* (or *Grammatices*) *Rudimenta: in usum regiae scholae Etonensis.* It was widely used outside Eton though not as extensively as the Eton Latin Grammar. Published at least as early as 1707; several revised editions appeared in the eighteenth century.

[61] Jane Wrather, 1732-1813, family friend from Masham. She married John Thirkill in 1775 and John Lonsdale signed the register. A tablet to her memory in Masham church refers to her patience under severe sufferings; she was blind. See Letters XVII and XL. She bequeathed £100 towards a Female Union Society in Masham parish.

duce him; but this is of no consequence as you may send Jo: along with him, after receiving Mr. Rogers Permission.

    I am in great haste to save the Post
        Yrs, truly
            J. Lonsdale

He must not return home for Easter Holidays. You should send for his Books.

XI

Monday afternoon, [11th March]

Dear Betty

    I got your letter this morning and am happy to find you all continue well. I am just returned from the Revenue Office where I have been to show to Mr. Harrison the rough Draft of my Letter to the S.G.[62] which he entirely approves of. I have particularly marked Pinkerton's particular Treachery to us, and his Character in general. The man he boarded with at Wombwell is Matthew Belk Carpenter.[63] For fear of our being called to Account for what I have said, desire Mr. Armer to call upon him, or upon any other Person likely to substantiate the charge, if it happens to be wanted. With respect to Joe's Question about the Soot. The Answer is this: If he thinks it is not too late and is likely to do good let him do it. If he is at all in Doubt about it, let it alone. Mr. Marris says there is a new Explanation of the Income Act coming out next week and that you need not be in Haste to deliver your Paper in. When I understand it, I will inform you. Tell me in your next what you think yourself we ought to put our income at. Jack's expences will not be allowed. The allowance is only so much a child. I will make the Enquiry about the Carriage and also about Col. Kearney: and the Charter Grammar—I like the situation of the Charter house very much, and in appearance think it preferable to Westminster. I see nothing to retract in my last hasty letter about sending Jack to Rogers. If we should be advised to send him to Eton after Easter, it would be 5 or 6 weeks before he could go and the being

---

[62] i.e. Letter XII.
[63] Wombwell was part of Darfield parish and many of the Belk family are buried there.

out of Training all that time might make him appear to a Disadvantage. Tell Mr. Rogers that it was my Intention to have begged this Favor of him before I went from home; and that my long absence was entirely unexpected. Mr. Wilkinson's Bill too should be paid and his Books brought home. Get over the business as handsomely as you can. I am sorry to impose it upon you. Instead of being called Sunk Island, one would take it to be Paradise. Mr. H. told me today another application was sent in last Saturday.[64] I am determined to follow your Idea of not losing it, if even 4 or 500 L per annum can be cleared by it. But I chuse to the last minute we can safely to stand our ground upon Mr. Whitelock's Estimate. I have requested the S.G. to dismiss me at least before Easter. I have invited Mr. Harrison to dine with us on Friday or Saturday and promised to teaze them no more. Having settled about Jack's going to Rogers, there is not so much haste in going to Eton. Indeed I cannot go to morrow having my letter to write and Mr. Marris being determined to leave me. I had written to Jackson and received from him the Account of Stubbings' Treachery—Mr. Thomson would give it up but Iveson and Stubbing refuse to do it.[65] If you know an honest man, love him truly.

J.L.

P.S. I have bought a Pocket Book for Jack but I don't know what is proper for the other two. Direct me.

XII
[to the Surveyor General]

London, March 12th 1799.

Sir,

Having been informed by Letters from Hull, that it is industriously reported by some of our opponents there, that the Crown Officers thought we had forfeited our Claim to the Renewal of Sunk Island Lease by unreasonable Delay; I beg Leave to lay before you the following Statement of Facts, of which our Solicitor has kept regular Minutes.

---

[64] Yeale had asked for more time on 9 March (Letter VIII, n. 51) and Thompson had increased his original offer on 6 March and again on 11 March.

[65] Perhaps an imprecise version of what Thompson had written to the Surveyor General (n. 53 above).

1796 Oct. 31—First application by the Lessees for a Renewal.

1797 Feb. —Petition for a Renewal delivered into the Treasury.

   April 15—Petition referred to the Surveyor General, and Survey ordered.

1798 Jan. 9—Mr. Whitelock's Report compleated.—

   May 5—Outlines of a Proposal sent to Mr. Johnson from the Land Revenue Office, with a copy of the Report.

     10—Lessees met at Bawtry to consider the Terms, and wished to have some Explanation.

     19—Letter received from the LRO with the Explanation.

   June 12—Mr. Johnson and Mr. Marris called at the LRO, to communicate their Sentiments on the Terms proposed; when Mr. Harrison informed them that Mr. Whitelock had been written to about some alterations in the Plan of Embankment, wch it was thought w^d be attended with less Risk, to stop at a certain point marked in the Plan, by wch Means the Part first embanked might yield some Profit whilst the remaining Embankment was making, and that Mr. W had been desired to send in a supplementary Report on that Head: And Mr. Johnson and Mr. Marris also desired to be informed as to the time the Lessees might expect to hold the unembanked Part Rent-free to compensate them for laying down their Money wch they stated they were willing to do.

   July —Waited for this supplementary Report, and likewise for a further August opinion from Mr. Dyson an Engineer employed by the Lessees, who was at that time engaged with other Business and c^d not attend them.

   Aug. 21—Mr. Johnson left London and proposed to Mr. L and Mr. O to meet them upon the Island in September, to take a View thereof and to examine the intended Lines of Embankment, but on Mr. J's coming into the Country and finding himself engaged unexpectedly by Business relating to his own Family, they were unable to proceed to the Island until October.

   Oct. 31—Mr. L, Mr. J and Mr. O set off to view the Island, and had proceeded as far as Thorne, where they met a letter from their Tenant signifying that on Acc[oun]t of the State of the Tides the Island c^d not be viewed at that time.

Nov. 12—Mr. L, M, J and Mr. O viewed the Island.

24—Letter sent from the R.O. to Mr. Marris at Bawtry requesting the Lessees to give their final Answer, wch Letter miscarried, and Mr. Marris has not yet rec^d it.

Dec. 3—The Lessees met at Bawtry to arrange to digest the observations they had made upon the Island, and to draw up their Memorial.

1799   Jan. 9—Rec^d a letter from the LRO inclosing a copy of the Letter above referred to of the 24th Nov:, and wch on acc[oun]t of the former Miscarriage was the very first Intimation to the Lessees of the S G's pressing for their Answer to the Proposals, or any other Applicants for the Lease having come forward.

If you will have the goodness to examine the Statement, and also to take into your Consideration the great Expence the Lessees have already been to in preparing for the proposed Embankment, I cannot entertain a Doubt of your Judgement being abundantly convinced, that they have been in good earnest in this Business, and really exerted themselves to the very utmost of their Power.

Will you here pardon me for expressing to you the very improper Behaviour of our present opponent James Pinkerton. At the very time he was soliciting to be our Engineer, and under that Sanction was permitted to view the Island, and obtain Possession of our Plans, he was basely and treacherously forming a Party at Hull to counteract and defeat our Success. It is very unpleasant to me to accuse any Man, but as James Pinkerton has lived for some time last past in my own Neighbourhood; I have the best Authority to say, that he is a Person of very loose Character, and has run into Debt wherever he has been concerned.

May I presume to add, that your former Kindness in excusing my earlier Attendance in Town encouraged me to hope that I shall be enabled to return to the Duties of my Church at least before Easter with the Satisfaction of having bro[ugh]t this Business to a happy Termination? It is with great Reluctance I give you this additional

Trouble, after the very kind Attention you have paid to our repeated applications to You.

I am,
Sir,
Your most obliged humble Serv[an]t,
J. Lonsdale

XIII

Eton Friday evening
[March 15]

Dear Betty

I did not receive your letter till last night, having been dining for
the first time with Mrs. Thirkhill. But it determined me to set off
immediately for this Place. And very lucky was it for me for I found
the School breaking up and the Masters setting off Tomorrow
Morning on their respective excursions. Dr. Heath behaved to me
with wonderful Humility and goodness and which nothing but
superior Knowledge can inspire. He advised me to send John here
April 1st not later than Apr. 3rd., the School opening on the 1st.
No time he says is to be lost and he will enter him senior of his
year, that is the First after the Easter Vacation. And [so] much
is the value of Time he says that it would be of great Service to him
to be instructed immediately "in the Formation of the Tenses
according to the Eton Greek Grammar". Jack will know what he
means, and he would have him only to make himself very Perfect
in *that* Part now; the time not permitting to do any more. As
therefore you set your Face against his going to Rogers' House
let him ride his Poney every Morning and return at Night. You
must send a Handsome Note to Mr. Rogers and ask it from me
as a particular Favor. If he has time to improve him in writing
Latin Verses so much the better, as it is here particularly expected.
To convince you that you must not lose an hour in doing this, I
sit down to write to you the moment I am come in to the Inn. I will
go tomorrow Morning to the Boarding House and send you a list
of Necessaries: being to return to London by 9 o'clock coach.

"5 or 10 shirts and as many pairs of stockings will be sufficient,
2 coats wasecoats and Breeches will do; a 3rd old sute would do
no harm. If the materials were sent to be made up at Eton perhaps
it might please a Boy better! But I think this absurd, our own

Taylor being just as good as theirs. I have paved the Way for his going without me. If unfortunately I am confined here till the time, he may come to me in London.

I have just got your last Letter. I delivered in to the S.G: Pinkerton's Character. If there be occasion for it, we must defend ourselves as well as we can. Take no more trouble about him. I wrote to Ramsey to apply to Mrs. Midgeley but he can do nothing. If things call for it, I must think of Mrs. Harcourt. You had better send to Worsbro[66] than trouble Mr. Wood too much. I have bought a Greek Grammar at Eton but Mr. Rogers will lend him one for the present. I fear you are wrong in stating the Deduction for 2 chil. 40£ and for one 15£. Is the Deduction to be taken from the Income or the Tax? I will endeavour to inform myself. I like Eton very well. The Boys I saw looked charmingly. I wish John to go as prepared as possible. The Business of the Island is at a Dead Pause. I must see it out. My Head and Stomach are both ill with riding alone in the Coach.

[There is no signature]

XIV

Monday 3 o'clock
[18 March]

Dear Betty

I went this morning to breakfast with Mr. Hardcastle and on my return went with my Cousin Mr. Beridge who is here, but going home tomorrow, to examine the Coach Repositories. No carriage,[67] not worse for wear can be got for less than 80 or 100 Guineas. We have seen one for 100£ which Beridge admires very much and thinks entirely equal to his own which cost 145£. It is painted yellow, which, he says, is the only colour that will stand.

---

[66] Two miles south of Barnsley.

[67] See Letters XXIII, XXIX, XXXIV, XXXV. It appears that the Lonsdales wanted to buy a carriage and give their chair in part exchange. The chair, very little longer than a sedan chair, would have had a small chariot body with the door in front and with a window on each side. It was hung on two lofty wheels with long shafts and would be drawn by one horse. This chair was to be exchanged for a more comfortable post chaise, a four-wheeled vehicle with the two back wheels higher than those in front and which would require two horses. Such carriages could cost up to 500 guineas though the more usual price was between £100 and £200. Advertisements in local papers of the period show that second hand post chaises were sold for prices similar to that mentioned in Letter XXXIV.

I hope you would receive this morning my letter from Eton,[68] recommending Jack to be sent to me here on 1st or 2nd April and in the meantime to be learning under Rogers "the Formation of the tenses in the Eton Grammar" and to practise himself in Latin Verses: the little time allowing for nothing more. I sent you directions about the Clothes. Mr. Hardcastle approves entirely of what I have done. I have seen an Answer from the S.G. to my last Letter to him,[69] vindicating ourselves from the Charge of unnecessary Delay, and praying to be released before Easter. I will quote for your Perusal a Part of it, flattering at the same time it is very discouraging. After saying that the Determination was not with him but with the Treasury he proceeds "I shall only add that your Letters and your Conversation on the subject of your Application have on every occasion been so fair, moderate and sensible, that on your Acc[oun]t I uniformly wished that you might find it for your Interest to offer such Terms, as that those who have the Power might find it consistent with their Duty to agree to the Acceptance of them. And I am very sorry that you are put to the inconvenience of remaining so long in Town: but it is not really in my Power to do anything to remove that Inconvenience". This you will say is very handsome: but the misfortune is, that it is said to be the opinion of the Lords of the Treasury, that they are bound to favor the Highest Bidder. So that we have the Preference, it may not be worth our having. I have written to Outwith and Welch[70] for their final Determination.

If I have got into a Scrape about Pinkerton, it is too late to be amended. I can only plead my being informed so and you must make out my case as well as you can. Our success remaining so precarious, it will be Policy not to talk on the Subject. Mr Hardcastle thinks Mrs. Harcourt can do us no good and I am advised not to teaze Mr. Smythe any more, having never acknowledged the receipt of my Letter to him. Mr. Pitt is the *great* man and will act as he thinks proper. What do you mean by going smart? I am

[68] Letter XIII.

[69] The Surveyor General wrote to Lonsdale 16 March disclaiming the report (Letter XII) that officers of the Crown had said that the lessees had forfeited Sunk Island by their delay.

[70] William Gylby Welch 1764-1805, grandson of Ruth, daughter of William Gylby, and one of the lessees. He died at Bawtry and there is a memorial inscription in Everton church where many of William Gylby's descendants are commemorated.

shaved and my wig dressed every morning. Do you wish me to
have a new Sute, Hat, Wig, etc. If I could avoid it, I should think it
as prudent, but you know I shall follow your Advice. If you have
not wrote before this arrives, I shall hope to hear from you again.
Perhaps it would be only Civil to see Geo Dyson's son. Let me know
where he lives. It might not be improper to enquire on what Terms
the young man at Worsbro' would undertake my Duty for me. If
we get the Island, Mr. Marris advises me to attend to everything
myself. Our money yet remains in Mr. Bolland's Hands, having
yet had no occasion for any. When Jack is admitted 12 or 15 G. will
be wanted. I begin to be quite tired out. God's blessing on you
and the children.

Yours most faithfully,
J. Lonsdale.

XV

Thursday Morn. 11 o'clock.
[March 21]

My dear Betty

Your very welcome Letter has just found me in my Room after
Breakfast musing about my very uncertain and unpleasant Situa-
tion. Your being all well, and approving of what I have done at
Eton, raises my Spirits and I sit down to give it as perfect an
Answer as I can.

My Return is now entirely uncertain: and may be a month
longer as well as a Week. I have told the S.G. in Answer to his last
Letter, that certainly my Duty to my wife and children will induce
me to remain in London, as long as I can be of any Service to the
Cause I have in Hand. Pinkerton has given up his Pretensions;
Stubbing and Iveson who is Mayor of Hedon[71] and has most
Interest in the Borough there, are the present formidable opponents.
Their offers are of such a Nature, that Harrison told me yesterday
in Confidence that they had applied again to Whitelock for his
opinion.[72] It appears to me, that nothing now can be done by

---

[71] See Letters VIII, n. 50 and IX, n. 56.
[72] Whitelock replying 14 March to a query from the Surveyor General about
the high offers he had received for the island advised terms "which shall be a
stimulus to spirited conduct" and recommended appropriate covenants in the lease
as safeguards.

us but I wait for the final Determination of the Lords and S.G. as
they must surely give us a Refusal, to immediately close with the
Terms proposed, if we safely can. Mr. Marris has written to me to
assure me, that Mr. Outwith leaves it to my own Discretion to
do what I find expedient; and that he would not have us lose the
Island even at 25s. Acre. And I really feel it will not come lower,
which is 1200£ per Ann. more than we have yet offered. Don't
you pity me for being constrained to write such unpleasant things?
I have followed your Idea of writing to Stubbing.

I would have Jack to be here on the 2nd of April to go with me
to School the next Day: You must particularly specify the Coach,
and time and place of his Arrival.[73] I will have a Porter in Waiting
to bring him to me. As you say the Coach will be only one Night
out, if you deliver him to the Care of the Coachman, and engage to
give him a certain Reward upon bringing back a Ticket of his safe
Delivery. I hope there will be no Ground for Fear. With respect
to his Sute being made up at Eton, you may be right. I think I
explained to you that 2 would be sufficient, with the aid of perhaps
an old Coat. Though perhaps the Certificate of his Age may not
be wanted, it had better come along with him and I will leave it
in safe Hands. He is to board in the House of a Clergyman, a Minor
Canon,[74] who seems to be a very respectable Man. I thought this
would be a Satisfaction to you. He must not go to Eton later than
3rd April as Dr. Heath particularly specified that Day; and he
might perhaps lose Seniority by Neglecting it.

I will now proceed to the Income Bill, and after reminding
you of a few Particulars leave it entirely to yourself what to do for
the best. I did not tell you, I think before that a letter of Attorney
was given to Mr. Marris to receive the Rents of the Island till the
Works shall be completed. He was not willing to leave Bawtry
without, and considering the Temper and Situation of the other
Parties I thought it prudent not to oppose it. Now if the Lease is

[73] After slow progress in the use and efficiency of the coach service during the
first half of the 18th century, great improvements came with the beginning of the
mail coaches in 1786. The Royal Mail ran between London and Leeds through
Sheffield, Barnsley and Wakefield. The True Briton from Leeds was put on the
road in 1781. By the end of the century, this coach left the Old King's Arms in
Leeds at 5 a.m. and reached The Bull and Mouth, London at 3 p.m. next day
having called at Wakefield, Barnsley and Sheffield. See Letter XVIII, n. 83.

[74] Henry Blenkinsop 1766-? Son of Richard Blenkinsop of Oxford. Lincoln College,
M.A., 1789. John's housemaster at Eton.

taken, which at present seems to be the Wish of Outwith and Welch etc. I fear we shall be under a Necessity of calling out of the Funds very soon 1000£. or 1500£. which will of course diminish our Interest there. I shall also be under the absolute necessity of superintending the Embankment: that is rather you and I must take Lodgings as near as possible to S.I. at least for the Summer, which will involve in it the having a Curate also at Newmillerdam and will be an Expence in both places of not less that 60£. And you cannot do better than immediately to consider for me, how such Assistance can be got on the most reasonable terms. Suppose you was to apply to the Young Man at Worsboro, sounding him upon the subject, and if at liberty to engage him after Easter Sunday. I fear the School master at Cudworth[75] is engaged but he is a likely Man to give you information. Or could Armer get Darfield supplied. You will remember also, that we shall receive no improved Rents from the Pastures for at least a year and half. Have we 260 or only 25£ Interest from the Funds? I have an Idea that the Tax[76] will be taken from the original Income given in before the Deductions are made. The Taxes to be deducted are those upon Houses, Windows, male Servants, Carriages, Horses and Dogs; which were paid before the Contribution Act. But Mr Wood or Dixon will inform you. Your return need not be made till 5th April which will give you time enough to be clear about it. I would not have you teaze the Zouchs[77] only omit nothing proper. It is their Business to attend to you. I wish the Afternoon on Easter Sunday could be supplied. Can you get it done by any decent means? With Respect to Henry at Eton send to James Johnson of Sandall about him.

[75] Near Barnsley.
[76] Income Tax was introduced by Pitt for the first time in 1799. Those with an income of less than £60 per year were exempt. An elaborate scale of rates of payment was used for those whose incomes were between £60 and £200. Those with incomes of £200 and upwards paid tax at 2/- in the pound. Allowances were made for children of the tax payer's family. Previous to 1799 there had been taxes on houses, windows, male servants, carriages, horses and dogs. The Income Tax of 1799 was objected to on the score that it disclosed too much of the tax payer's circumstances and way of life. Drastic changes were made by Addington in 1805. See Letters XI, XXIII, XXIV, XXV, XXXIII, XXXV.
[77] Thomas Zouch 1737-1815. Son of Charles Zouch of Great Sandal, near Wakefield. Educated at Wakefield Grammar School and Trinity College, Cambridge. Friend and contemporary of John Lonsdale. He held the curacy of Chapelthorpe 1761-1772 together with a fellowship and tutorship at Cambridge. On the death of his brother in 1792 he succeeded to the estate at Sandal where he lived until his death.

He went to be Servant to a young gentleman under Mr. Briggs[78] and who is to be John's Tutor. He may be of Service to us. Write to me immediately, which is the greatest Consolation of

Yours affectionately

J.L.

XVI

[March 23]

My dear Betty,

I have just written two Letters, one to Mr. Welch and another to Mr. Ramsey: and though I don't know what I can add to my last, yet will try to do it.

I think Jack is much better improving in his Book, than being here. I never spend the evening out, nor leave my Room till the Post is come in. But still further, there is a Chamberlain standing all the Day and Evening in the Passage to the Hotel, a most steady good tempered Man, and to whom I have already commended the care of Jack half a dozen times already. You must give me the earliest Notice you can and I will take care to do my Part faithfully. You may send a letter in his pocket directed to me here. If you wish it, he shall certainly go to the Play: but the less Taste he has given him for this Place in my own opinion the better. I find Rhodes a very steady prudent man to all Appearance and very fit to be trusted: but I should rather chuse his returning by Birmingham if it can be found practicable. I have only been to his House once, but he has called here 3 or 4 time.

I have been to Col. Kearney's House. I find it covered with Notice to Lett. The Person I spoke to informed me they were still in Ireland, but expected at Waltham in the Spring. I will ask Mr. Johnson about Mr. Chalmers their Agent.

Mr. Briggs gave me the following list of Books for Jack to bring with him, if he has them "Ovid's Metamorph: Greek Test. Lexicon, Latin Dictionary—Gradus Caesar, Terence". If they are in any tolerable order, the bringing them will save expence.

Entrance to Boarding House	£6. 6. 0.
To Dr. Heath	£5. 5. 0.
Single bed	£5. 5. 0.

---

[78] Thomas Briggs 1767-1831. Scholar at King's from Eton in 1787. Assistant master at Eton 1792 1831. Died in Munich while travelling.

If a single room additional   £5. 5. 0.
If a study   £1. 1. 0.
Old clothes left as a Perquisite to servant, or one guinea per annum
in lieu of it.
An Oppidan 80 £.   Foundation 25 £.
   The Bell is ringing for the Letters. I will write again on Monday.
                    Yours always
                         J.L.
Sat. 6 o'clock.

XVII

                              Tuesday Afternoon   [March 26]
Dear Betty
   I did not write yesterday, expecting your letter today. I will
expect Jack then on Saturday Night and will take care to attend
at the Inn myself and bring him to my Lodgings in a Coach. I
will bespeak a warm Bed to be ready for him, after giving him
what you recommend. I will hope to hear your final instructions
on Saturday morning. If you wish him to see the Play on Monday
Night you have only to say so: I only fear giving him Cold. I have
been to ask Mr. Johnson about the Probability of his coming with
Mrs. Wood, whom he says you must not on any means wait for.
You should have mentioned Miss Raydon sooner. With respect to
the Income, I will leave it entirely to yourself. If you think 400£
would seem to little, give it in 500£. I have said everything that I can
say. With Respect to Deductions, you will be governed by your
Neighbour. You are sure, I should not like making a Schedule or
taking an oath. I have written to Mr. Whitelock but what good can
he do? He *has* been applied to *again* by the S.G. but is under In-
junction not to disclose secrets. I have letters both from Outwith and
Welch, advising me not to lose our Renewal for £25 or even £30
per annum for the unembanked Land: and that they will join me
in it and in giving all Security that shall be required. All this goes
up on the Idea of the Advantage of future embankments. Now if
we are determined to go to this Length surely we can not lose it:
as the preference on the highest terms *must* be given us. I have
waited twice on Mr. Coore who has received me with the warmest
Friendship. He has a little Boy exactly of Jack's Age now at Eton
and desires Jack to be introduced to him. He advises me to stand our

ground on the Surveyor's valuation and if rejected, to bring it before
Parliament. I have received a letter from Stubbing endeavouring to
explain away his Treachery and saying that we face other more
dangerous opponents which we have no Idea of. If you knew how
such Acc[oun]ts confound me and what perpetual Anxiety I have
been under, you would not reproach me but pity me. I make it my
continual Business and give up all Dinner Parties whatever. Parliament does not meet again till Wednesday week. I will then wait
upon Mr. Wilberforce and Mr. Smythe again and make my last
Effort. The Reason given by the S.G. for the Delay is that nothing
can be done till Mr. Pitt himself attends the Board and that he will
do as *he* pleases. It is too true that Col. Drummond fell down his
staircase and was thought to be in great danger (I have just heard
he is dead)[79] How uncertain is Life! There is one thing very unpleasant to be in the present Business which is its being so very
expensive. Mr. Johnson making a point of dining here almost
every Day and paying no regard to the Bill. When you think I
should come down tell me so. Mr. Harrison paid a Compliment the
other day to my great Patience. I told [him] my Wife would not
allow my Title to it. Let me now return to poor Jack who is constantly in my thoughts. Send me particular Directions about his
Clothes and everything. I don't doubt but he might be put up on the
Foundation this next Election but I thought both Dr. Heath and
Goodall[80] leaned to his remaining an Oppidan a year longer. It
will make the difference of perhaps 40£ or 30£. Mrs. Marsden is
too busy with her Family to receive Jack with convenience. And
Mrs. Thirkhill, who is almost blind, could by no means do it.
My love is not *less* to Henry[81] and Mary[82] because I have no time
to talk about them.
God bless you all.

J.L.

[79] According to the *Gentleman's Magazine* Col. Drummond fractured his skull
in his fall and died after a few days.
[80] Joseph Goodall 1760-1840, King's scholar from Eton 1779. Assistant master Eton
1783-1801, Headmaster 1802-1809, Provost 1809-1940, and Canon of Windsor.
[81] Henry Gylby Lonsdale 1791-1851. Second son of John Lonsdale. Educated at
Wakefield Grammar School and a governor from 1817-1825. Scholar of Jesus
College, Cambridge 1810, M.A. 1817. Rector of Bolton by Bowland 1826-30, vicar
of St. Mary's Lichfield, 1830-51. Married 1824 Anna Maria, daughter of John
Pemberton Heyward of Stanley Hall, Wakefield.
[82] Mary Lonsdale 1792-1810. Only daughter of John Lonsdale.

If I find upon enquiring that it will be more for his future Benefit not to go up on the Foundation so soon, the Expence shall not weigh with me.

XVIII

Thursday [March 28]

Dear Betty

You would receive another Letter from me this morning, in which I think you will find an Answer to everything contained in yours of this Day. I went yesterday to reconnoitre the Bull & Mouth Inn,[83] and find there very good Accommodation: so that, I shall dine there on Saturday and continue there till the True Briton Coach[84] comes in. And if Jack does not arrive then, I will repeat my Dining there till he does. I think the less he stays in London the better for Fear of being ill. I assure you this Idea dwells very strongly in my own mind. I have been so harrassed and agitated by the different Aspect of our present great Concern that the Amusements of this Place though innocent have lost their Power over me. I know you will say this is absurd, but one cannot always command ones Spirits as one would.

I will discharge the Guard's Expences: but perhaps you had better give the Reward upon the delivering a Note of his safe Arrival. At Eton I will endeavour to do all things to the best of my Power and Judgement. You have put me by your anxiety about my Appearance to the expence of ordering a new Sute of Clothes. As to the Hat and Wig, I will make them do as long as I can. My Shoes and Boots also proving thin and shabby. I have ordered a Pair of Half Boots which are General Morning Dress.

I expect Mr. Johnson calling upon me every minute to go to the Revenue Office. Though at present nothing can be done, yet a shew of Attendance must be kept up. Poor Johnson, who is too fond of Extra Eating and Drinking, thinks it right to ask Mr. Harrison

[83] Almost certainly this inn was the one of this name in St. Martin le Grand or Aldersgate, a well known stopping place for coaches going to and from the north. The name Bull and Mouth appears to be a corruption of Boulogne Mouth, the name first given to an inn in Holborn after Henry VIII took the town of Boulogne in France. Owing to the mispronunciation of Boulogne Mouth, in later times an ignorant sign painter represented the inn by a bull and huge human mouth.

[84] See Letter XV, n. 73.

to dine with us during the Reces[s] of Parliament. I will stop my Pen till our Return—I am just returned from the Revenue Office. am really afraid of telling you what we have heard; so suddenly changing have been our Reports. Mr. Harrison came down to us from the Surveyor General. He says, "Our Papers have at last got into Mr. Pitt's Hands, and we shall probably know his determination in a very little time. He thinks we are in no Danger from our Rivals, and that the worst will only be paying a little more rent for the new embanked Land at the End of 14 years, according to Mr. Whitelock's last Report".[85] He adds, "The whole matter depends upon Mr. Pitt and Mr. Fordyce. The other Lords dare not meddle with it". It appears then, if there be any sincerity in the office, that we are sure at last of getting our Renewal, though at a higher Rate. But I have been so frequently chastised by Disappointments that I cannot indulge great Confidence all at once. I touched on Stubbing's Ingratitude in hopes of him telling it to the S.G. I hope you have sent the Books I mentioned to you. I will write to you by the Guard or by the Monday Post and must then intreat you to have Patience with me till my Return from Eton which may not probably be till 5 or 6th April. I am to introduce John at Mrs. Coore's, and if I have time, I will do it also to Mr. Hardcastle, Mrs. Thirkill and Bolland. For God's sake, take care for full Duty at the Chapel if you can. With my best prayer for you. I am

yours
J.L

XIX

New Hummums
Sat: Morn.
[March 30th]

Dr.Mama

This is to acquaint you I am got so far on my journey very well. John is arrived safe, but did not reach London till after nine, and I had been waiting for him from 3 o'clock. I never was more anxious and impatient in my Life. The Coach you had put him into proved a very bad one, as well as the Horses. I have paid the Expences of the Guard, and given him 5ˢ Reward and 1ˢ for Fearnley and to him

[95] Whitelock in his reply to the Surveyor General (Letter XV, n.72) had reckoned the land to be enclosed as worth 15s. an acre for 14 years, 20-25s. afterwards.

to drink your Health. As a Proof of his being well this morning I will tell you where we have been, to Gloster St. to call upon Mr. Hardcastle, to Mrs. Thirkill's in St.James St. and to Mr. Johnson's in the Temple, and then down Oxford St. as far as the Park. We are now got to the Hummums, 4 o'clock, have given orders for a Veal Cutlet and Smelts and after that by your Desire intend going to Drury Lane. Mr. Johnson is going to meet Gen: Pott and Kennet and Annerley at 6 o'clock but as John did not wish to defer seeing The Play,[86] and besides wanted his Dinner, I have ordered it to be got ready immediately. John's Company is everything to me, and so long as he behaves well and attends to his Books, he shall never be refused anything proper for him. If he only minds his studies for one year till he gets high enough on the foundation there will be no Danger of his [not] getting forward, a Comfort to himself and an Honour to his Friends. I don't think Jack so unpolished to need an Apology. He walked in the streets to Day like an Officer. I will endeavour to observe as steadily as possible all your Directions. I will go to Eton on Wednesday morning, and after my Return write to you again. Take care of yourself and the dear Children, by doing which your ensure best the Happiness of

Yours most affectionately

J. Lonsdale

I cannot let this letter go without sending my Duty to you, Love to Henry and Mary.

J. Lonsdale jun^r.

XX

Sunday night
[March 31st]

My dear Betty

Having now put poor Jack to Bed, and who by my particular Desire sleeps very near to me, I return to my Chamber to inform you how we have spent the Day: As soon as we had finished our Breakfast, I took him to hear the Sermon at Westminster Abbey; after which we examined most of the monuments and went through the Cloisters to Westminster School: But it was so piercingly cold, that really we could not bear it, but immediately took

---

[86] The Stranger. See Letter XX.

a coach for Clapham, where we have spent a very comfortable Day with the Bollands, who are a most agreable and respectable Family. I will give you a Proof of Mrs. Bollands[87] great Tenderness to your Son. She expressed herself extremely pleased with his sense of gravity and taking Notice of one of his teeth growing very awkwardly, voluntarily offered to attend us Tomorrow morning to a principal Dentist in Town, whom she employed for her own Children: and who of course would give his opinion without a fee. I thought this extremely friendly in her and have engaged to meet her at 12 o'clock. This will prevent me from waiting upon Mrs. Coore before Tuesday and on Wednesday we go to Eton.

John is exceedingly pleased with London and called me back again into his Chamber to Night to beg of me to inform you, that he had seen Mrs. Siddons last Night in the Stranger.[88] He was very attentive and at the Close of a very pathetic Story feelingly observed "It is a well written Description"! Who should come do you think into my Room this morning by 7 o'clock without any knocking but your Son John, full drest, gaiters on, all ready for walking to see the W—.[89] It is enough he says for People in the Country to be idle, and lie long in Bed.

As my wardrobe is now increased, I should suppose my small Portmanteau would be [in]sufficient to bring everything Home. Be so good as to think about this, and give instructions what sort of Trunk will be likely to be useful to us in future. You had best fix the exact size of it.

I have received Letters again from Marris and Outwith encouraging me to take the Lease even at 25^s per A[cre]; but I hope we shall surely gain it upon more reasonable terms. I now hope we shall know our Fate very soon. What must I say too abut the Duty? Jack says Mr. Wood has promised to do it. But have you enquiried at Worsbro', Cudworth,[90] etc. for Assistance if wanted? I forget to mention Mr. [illegible] at Keresforth Hill,[90] who assisted me in

---

[87] Wife of John Bolland of Clapham. See note 21, Letter III.

[88] Sarah Siddons 1755-1831. Daughter of Roger and Sarah Kemble. Born at the Shoulder of Mutton public house, Brecon. Her father being a strolling actor, she early performed on the stage. In 1773, married a young actor, William Siddons and became much sought after and famous both at Drury Lane and in the Provinces. On 24th March, 1798, she appeared as the original Mrs. Hallam in the Stranger. This was one of her greatest parts and she played it twenty-six times during that season.

[89] Illegible.

[90] Places near Barnsley.

Letting the Land at Dodworth.[90] We must not be too hard upon
Wood. You must judge for me. I have no objection to your giving
in our Income as 500 L. if you think it best. Write to me for
Friday or Saturday. Jack talks without ceasing and joins in Love
with J.L.

XXI

Thursday Night
[April 4th]
7 o'clock

My dear Betty
   I am just returned from Eton, and as I cannot but sympathize
with you in your Anxiety upon this Subject, sit down immediately
to satisfy it. We set off yesterday morning by 8 o'clock and without
Breakfast, but contrived to get a Cup of Tea upon the Road,
while the Horses were changing. Dr. Heath received his new
Scholar with great Affability, took him kindly by the Hand, and
asked him to enter his own Name in his Book, promising to place
him as high as he properly could. We then went to his Tutor Mr.
Briggs, who is a very sedate, sensible man. He asked John to con-
strue a Verse in the greek Testament, and to make him a Latin
Verse, in which John did not acquit himself quite as well as I
could have wished, being a little confused in his memory. He
acknowledged however, that he seemed to have been well taught,
and hoped he would do very well. In short I found what I always
thought before, that John had been neglected in Composition. I was
determined however to fight the Battle thro, as well as I could, and
took John with me to breakfast with him this morning. I assured
him, that John was studious, and by no means deficient in Abilities
and he has promised to give him every assistance in his Power.
We dined and spent the Evening at Mr. Blenkinsop's who is a
very pleasant and agreeable man, and has engaged to adopt John
for his Son. Mrs. Blenkinsop lies in, and consequently I did not
see her. But what will you say when I tell you that we had the
Honor of drinking tea with Dr. Dodsworth the present resident
Canon at Windsor![91] He had heard of my having been there and

[90] Place near Barnsley.
[91] Frederick Dodsworth 1738-1821. Second son of John Dodsworth of Thornton
Watlass near Masham. He attended Sedbergh School and was admitted to Christ's
College, Cambridge in 1756. He proceeded to the degrees of M.A. in 1764. D.D.

very obligingly left Word for me to call upon him when I came again. He is related to the Vice Provost of Eton and said he would do John any Service in his Power.

Mr. Briggs has his mother and sisters along with him, who are very respectable People. I think she was sister to the Bishop of London. He speaks of Mr. Holdsworth of Normanton as his particular Friend and if we could procure a Letter from Mr. Holdsworth in our Favor it might perhaps have a good effect. It might perhaps excite more attention to him, but the sooner the better. They enquiried also after Miss Rickaby. But I must tell you something that will both vex you and please you at the same time. They are going to have at Eton what they call the Montem,[92] great Festival once in 3 years and all the Boys are to appear in Scarlet: so that the Cloth you sent must be brought back again. This will certainly be an additional expence but must I find necessarily be complied with. Eton is indeed a most charming Place for a school,—can anything but Expence be alledged against it. I am happy in adding that John upon the whole has behaved exceptionally well, and is indeed a most sensible agreable child. He seemed most pleased with Eton. He will write to you in a Fortnight's time. I am sorry for the Death of poor Cutforthey. He has been a short lived Possessor of his new Improvements. I hear nothing from Mr. Pitt. I am very impatient and yet fear to irritate by showing it too much. When I do come back, must I return through Bawtry and settle my Business or come directly home and go to Bawtry afterwards? Never mind Armer's rudeness. Is there any chance of getting an Assistant?

Yrs. J.L.

John was wonderfully delighted with the Plays but, before the conclusion, sank down asleep upon my shoulder. It was hard work to leave him behind me; but we both of us acted our Parts as well as could be expected.

---

in 1784. He was vicar of Spennithorne, Yorkshire, a parish in Wensleydale not far from Masham, 1778-1821, and made a canon of Windsor in 1782. (*Alumni Cantabrigenses*).

[92] In the programme for the Montem festival on June 8th, 1802, Lonsdale is listed as a Poleman.

XXII

Monday Afternoon
[April 8]
5 o'clock

My dear B,

I am unwilling to omit answering your letter of this Day, tho'
I don't see I have much to say upon it. I have been pleasing myself
to-Day with the hope of your Receipt of John's good journey to
Eton. Everything seemed to succeed to the utmost of my wishes;
and I really don't know whether anything more can be done for
him. If you think my writing to Mr. Sumner would be taken well,
and might be of service, I will certainly do it immediately: and for
the same Reason you should request Mrs. Kearney to obtain a
Letter from Major Thackary. But really both Dr. Heath and Mr.
Briggs seemed to be willing to do everything for him. It is a good
thing however to be on the safe side and perhaps, it would be
wrong to neglect it. Your Brother James[93] called upon me on his
way to Ireland. He says he takes it for granted that Col. Kearney
is at Londonderry and must in all Appearance remain there for
some time. You are a very good monitor to me; and if I find occasion for it, I shall certainly apply to Mr. Wilberforce. I wrote on
Saturday to the Surveyor General[94] entreating him to restore me
to my Family, and I shall wait very anxiously for his Answer. You
will not, I think find fault with me, when I tell you that I introduced Jack to Mr. Harrison at the Revenue Office: He said he was
a fine Boy, and promised to call upon him at Eton. It was very
lucky I did not teaze Mr. Smythe. He has been much indisposed,
his case, as far as I could understand, is a surgical one. This came
out in conversation with Dr. Heath at Eton, who was observing to
me, that his Son lately gone to Cambridge was amazingly clever.
Dr. Heath said he was particularly intimate with Lady Georgiana.[95]
Would it be right for me to make Enquiries after him? Give me
your advice in your next letter. If Mary is intended to go to School,

---

[93] James Steer, 1758- Son of Charles Steer a merchant of Westgate Wakefield
who died 1786 and is buried at Sandal, and his second wife Sarah Allott. Half
brother to Elizabeth Lonsdale.

[94] This letter has not been located.

[95] Smythe's wife and daughter of the third Duke of Grafton. See Letter XXV.

I think you had better send her immediately. She is as little likely to get cold there, as at Home. With respect to writing to the Coach Maker at Durham, I wish you most sincerely to follow your own wishes. If you would be happier by changing the Chair for a Chaise, I promise you most cordially to join you in it. Every thing for your real Good shall be ever nearest to my Heart. Pay every Civility to Mrs. Cutforthey, whether he has left you anything or not. Let not Resentment destroy Politeness. I called this morning on Mrs. Wood and Miss Bayldon. Miss B. looks charmingly. I was obliged to apologise as well as I could, by saying I did not know but Mrs. W. was gone into the country with Mr. Wood. You must not write under the Seal: I cannot see clearly the Size of the Trunk. Send it separately at the Bottom of your Paper. I fear there is time enough. Do you know of any Person wanting a title? I am called down to Dinner.

Yours faithfully. J.L.

XXIII

Thursday Noon
[April 11]

My dear B.

Since I last wrote to you it has occured to me, that perhaps I answered the question about a Chaise in too general Terms. I will endeavour now to give it as fair and liberal a Description as I can. I will reckon the Price of the Chaise 100£: for I would not have a shabby one. We will call this then only 5£ annual Diminuation of our Income. The additional Tax 5£, the contingent Expences let us rate as low as possible at 10£ = 20£ total. This you see is but a small sum: if we can do without it for the next 3 years. I think I told you before, that the Rents of the Island are sequestered during that term for the intended Improvements. I should hope 1000£ more taken out of the Funds would be equal to our Share of the whole Expence. And at the end of that term, as far as I can judge, we should be likely to receive from the Island about 600£ a year for our own share for the next 8 years: after which our Rent for the new embanked Part is to commence and we must take our chance for the Advance of Rent we could make and which Mr. Outwith seems to form sanguine hopes of. This is the best explanation I can give you of the Business, having almost puzzled myself in doing it.

Give it for me a critical examination, with your opinion about it. Now it appears to me from this Statement, that we shall be pinched for the next 3 years, which is a very unpleasant Idea at our Time of Life: but which I see no Remedy for, but by borrowing 5 or 600£ or selling it out of the Stocks as we happen to want it: and which perhaps would be the better way. The Inference I wish to draw from what I have said is this: If you consider a Chaise as likely to promote your Health and Comfort, I would recommend it you to have one at present, before that Health and Comfort be taken from you.

I really think you have given in our Income too high. In my own opinion Darfield should not be above 60, Chapelthorpe 100£, and the Pastures 80£. This will certainly be increased by a higher Tax the next year: Great Caution should [MS damaged] I went again to the Revenue Office yesterday and saw the Surveyor General. He received me with his usual Politeness and pitied my long confinement in town. He said Mr. Douglas[96] a Lord of the Treasury had taken our Papers into the Country, which had prevented Mr. Pitt from seeing them; but promised to give us an Answer in a few Days. Would not this be an Exercise for even your boasted Patience? If you have not been used to consider me as a Philosopher, I beg you will prepare yourself to receive me in that character. You see how uncertain my Return is, and specifying my Attendance on the Sunday following and which at present is very unlikely you must hunt about for Assistance. Have you enquired at Worsbro, Stainbro etc.[97] There is a little Drawback which we never thought of in giving in our Income 5 or 6£ paid annually to my Father's old Servant. I begin to think that 30£ will be quite enough for us to pay. If it is not too late give me your opinion about it.

Yours

J. Lonsdale

[96] Sylvester Douglas 1743-1823. After studying medicine and then law, he was admitted to Lincoln's Inn 1771, called to the bar 1776, and K.C. 1793. He became a member of the Privy Council in 1794, an M.P. in 1795, and was appointed a lord of the Treasury in 1797. Created Baron Glenbervie in 1800, he was Surveyor General of Woods and Forests 1803-6, and from 1807 until 1810 when, the offices of Surveyor General of Land Revenue and Surveyor General of Woods and Forests being united, he became first chief commissioner of the combined offices. See Introduction p. 35 n. 85.

[97] Near Barnsley.

XXIV

Saturday 13 Apr.

My dear B.

I have received your last Letter and sit down as usual, to notice everything in it I think useful. You say you have written to Miss Rickaby, whom Mrs. Briggs enquired after: but Mr. Holdsworth was spoken of by Mr. Briggs as *his* particular Acquaintance and seems to be the Person, whose Letter to Mr. Briggs might be of Service to us. Mr. Briggs Jack's Tutor was not Curate at Methley, but only Brother to him. If I have not made a mistake myself, Mr. Wood is wrong about the Boys on the Foundation having no Tutor. I gave consent to Jack's remaining an Oppidan till the Election twelve months, tho' the principal Reason I could find was to prevent his being too much fagged. I knew you would not like that. But it will cost us 40 or 50 £ more. Mr. Wood is indeed very good to us but I fear much to abuse his goodness. You must be a Judge of that. You would receive a Letter from me yesterday, explaining as clearly as I could the Extent of our Income for the next 3 years if we get the Island and which I am sure you will join me in lamenting as too contracted: and see the Necessity of paying no higher Tax to Government, than what Equity and Conscience compel us to do. And in my own opinion it will be prudent to act with such Caution as that no future Appeal may be necessary. With respect to any Tax for the Island, it appears to me it ought to be done collectively by the Lessees together, if it shall be found necessary. But of this I am not a perfect judge. It will perhaps pull in the Tenants. The Expences about the Island incurred before and now will, I fear, be very heavy and must be defrayed immediately as soon as our present Business is done. So that to talk about investing in the Funds now is sadly premature. I have already drawn from Mr. Bolland 50£ since Mr. Marris went. Mr. Ramsey has about 100£ in his Hands belonging to our Share, and which we may draw for, when we please. The next Rents, as I said before, are sequestered. I feel with you that this is by no means a pleasant Idea. But there was no Remedy. The chance of Major Thackray's doing Service to Jack is by writing to Dr. Goodall or Heath or Briggs to push him as high as they can or by giving Advice about him. I will defer my Application to Mr. Sumner till nearer offering for the Foundation. I did not desire Mr. Briggs or Mr. Blenkinsop to write to me in London but I dare say you will have a letter in 2 or 3 weeks' time. How could I suppose I should continue here so long? No News yet from the Treasury. If you think it will be proper for me to call upon Mr. Horncastle send me word what No. he lives at. I have dined with the Ashmores who are all very well, and yesterday dined with Mr. Graham, Mr. Hardcastle's relations. I wish you would come up to me with a Bottle of your good Spirits. I have only this moment got your letter. I will write to Mr. Sumner according to your Recommendation. Where is Mrs. Martindale's Daughter? You never mentioned her before. I was going this morning to the Revenue Office but will forbear till Monday from your idea of not teazing them too much. Mr. Hardcastle and his Friend Graham have a bad opinion of our Business. You said in your former Letter I had better let the Trunk be unbought. Tell me positively if you thing I had better have it. Tell Jo: to push his work in the Fallow as forward as the weather will permit him. I have spoken to Dyson about Hope. If I find on Monday, that our Business is not likely to be done in a week or two, must I come Home.

Yours always   J. Lonsdale

XXV

Wednesday 17th April

My dear B.

I have just received your Letter and am very happy in hearing you all continue well. Having heard nothing from you a Post or two, I began to be very impatient. I don't know what I can say more about the Taxes. I wish to do what is right and at the same time to make the Payment not too heavy for my real Income. My Land on Woodmore is not worth more than 20s. per A. And with Respect to the Pastures you must reckon no more than the Average of the last 3 years deducting a Sufficiency for Leasehold. Mr. Whitelock knows where I am, and if he does not chuse to call on me, it would not be prudent for me to force him to it. In his Answer to my Letter, he says he is bound to Secrecy and refers me to Mr. Harrison. If you had any idea of the unpleasant Nature of my present Application, you would not say I am depressed without cause. It is the third Day I have attended successively at the Revenue Office with-

out any Effect. Yesterday I had an Audience of the S.G. in which
he pretended to communicate to me in *confidence* what Mr. Pitt
intended to do, but said he would see him again in the Morning
and to-day give me a final Answer. When I waited on him at his
own Hour half-past one, I was desired by Mr. Harrison to call on
Friday. But I heard enough yesterday to convince me we shall
be used very cruelly. A Mr. Worsop,[98] and Wood and Mr. Harrison
says Pinkerton are connected with them, have made an offer to
government to pay the whole Rent before proposed to us at the end
of 8 years, *immediately*, and to make the Embankment Buildings
etc. at their own unaided Expense. We are to have the Preference at
the same Rate. Upon my urging our particular merits, he said Mr.
Pitt would allow us about 70 £ p.Ann. for Mrs. Gylbey's Suit, and
5 p.cent on the whole value as old Lessees i.e. about 150£. If we
will give up the Island at the End of our Lease without injury, they
will give us 1000£. Now what do you think of all this unfeeling
Behaviour? I have wrote yesterday to Mr. Marris and Outwith for
their final opinion, whether I shall accept or reject the Renewal
on such Terms. I am myself strongly inclined to accept it, from a
Hope posibly of future Benefit to my Children. But let me ask you,
would you hear all this with unabated Patience and would you find
yourself in the Humour to go up and down the Town, seeking
whom to call upon? I will join you however in your most excellent
Sentiment, that if my wife and children do but remain well I shall
be happy with [illegible]. You will collect then from the Face of
[things] that I shall most probably be able to return home to day
sennight but I will write again on Monday or Tuesday next which
you will get on Thursday morning with my certain Determination.
Mr. Johnson never goes along with me now to the office being
entirely worn out. I rejoice in the good News of poor Jack. I did
not desire him or them to write to me here, being so very uncertain and fearing it might unsettle him: I hope he is placed pretty
high. I have not yet wrote to Mr. Sumner, but if you continue to
think it proper, will not fail to do it. As you make no mention of

---

[98] See Letter VI, n. 41. Worsop's memorial, handed in at the Treasury 23 February,
offered to lay out the £9,000 or thereabouts required for improvements at Sunk
Island and offered an annual rent of 3,000 guineas, with deductions of £1,600 in
the first year and £800 in the second as the embankments and other works would
not be completed before the end of that time. With further allowances for the
cost of Whitelock's survey, building a chapel and other adjustments, this would
produce the figures set out in Letter XXX.

the Trunk, perhaps you have dropt the idea of it. The Direction
to Jack at Mr. Blenkinsops, Eton, Windsor will be sufficient. As
he is such a young correspondent, you must write nothing to him
but what will show well again. You may add something with it
to Mr. Blenkinsop and Mrs. B. that if anything is wrong or deficient in his clothes it shall be made up. I asked Mr. Fordyce
yesterday how Mr. Smythe did. His answer was he had never seen
him since the Death of Lady Georgiana: a plain proof he had not
been at the Treasury Board. He never returned any Answer to my
Note. You may mention to John the Books that we use by Name,
perhaps he may tell Mr. Briggs.

Yours truly
J.L.

XXVI

Thursday 25th Apr.

Dear Betty

I receive the News of poor Henry's being better with great
Thankfulness. For God's Sake take a prudent Care of him, not
keeping him too warm and by that means exposing him to a
second taxing Cold. Poor Lad, bad Scholar as he is, he is still very
dear to me! You must for the same Reason keep a careful eye upon
Mary. I went yesterday to the Bank to change our Stock. If I can
believe the Broker who seems a very [illegible] man, it is a very
good Business done. I have £5200 New 5% Cents for 5,100£ old
and £17.13.6. into Pocket. But then the Interest will not be due
till Michalmas. The great Advantage, as the Broker explains it, is
that you are entitled to take your money out at Par 2 years after
the Peace, with the option of so much 3 p. cents as the money will
purchase at £75, and which may eventually be worth 4 or 500 £.
You have also a Power of purchasing in the Long Annuities at a
certain Rate and which may under some circumstances be useful
and they are not liable to Redemption like the old. Tell Jo. to sow
red clover and to be careful to get it good. He may sow Tartureen
Oats in the other close and do anything else which is wanted with
Respect to Hedging etc. It does not appear that Wright or Gee have
any concern with the Island. The Persons now said to be at the Top
of the Bidding[99] gave in their Proposals soon after our Coming

[99] i.e. Worsop.

to Town and are entirely speculators in the Business. One of them Wood, is a Land Valuer, and probably impels the Rest. If Pinkerton is concerned with them, it is probably no more than as an Engineer. Mr. Johnson spent the evening with me, and has made my Head ache. I have persuaded him to attend me to the Revenue Office To Day and I will afterwards tell you the Result of it. It seems to be a clear Point, that we must make a Contract for our Lease, as cheap as possible if we afterwards dispose of it. I have written to Mr. Whitelock to know if he is soon coming to Town. I would not have you enclose any more Pieces of Paper in your Letters as one of these has been charged a treble Letter. The poor Chamberlain is extremely shocked with the Number and Charge of my Letters, and asked me very anxiously the other Day if you was not indispoed. I have got new lenses put into your spectacles. I am really puzzled about the Taxes and will advise with you when I get home. I have seen Mrs. Harvey, who is very well. I have engaged to dine with her on Sunday. Mrs. Batty has also sent me an Invitation to dine with her which it will give me Pleasure to have it in my power to do. I return from the Revenue Office, as you say you yourself felt upon my former Letter, with a heavy heart. No relaxation whatever will be made in our Terms. I have Reason now to suppose with you that W— may be concerned as it appears that Mr. Smythe's opinion [is] against us. I have determined to accept an option of the Lease and if it does not appear to be worth holding, to sell it as well as we can. The minute of the Treasury is to be sent to me To-Night or To-morrow.[100] I will then solicit a last Interview with the S.G. and take my Leave. If then no unforseen Alteration takes place, I shall be at home before Sunday Sennight. What Day I cannot fix upon but it shall be the earliest in my Power, or Thursday or Friday. If any further Cause of Delay occurs and really there is no arguing about what may occur, you shall hear from me on Thursday or Saturday morning; and if you still find that I am detained longer, you must get the Duty done as well as you can. Perhaps Mr. Sanderson might come from Bretton in the Afternoon if he had time to give Notice in the morning for no Duty there. If then this should happen to become necessary you must send Jo: to Bretton to the Clerk with a

[100] Long wrote from the Treasury to the Surveyor General 25 April to acquaint him with the terms on which a new lease would be granted to the existing lessees. For the terms see Letter XXVII, n. 102.

Note on the Saturday and which would enable you to give Geo: Dyson timely Notice for no Morning Duty at the Chapel. But if you can get the whole Duty done, it will be better. But as the Face of things now is there will be no occasion. I wrote to Outwith a few days ago but shall not wait for his Answer. Mr. Johnson advises me to come by Bawtry: but I am determined to lose no time in getting home. Except you see some particular Reason for writing again to me immediately on the Receipt of this, you had better write no more. I have not yet determined whether I shall come in the Mail or the Duncan.[101]

God preserve you all!
J. Lonsdale

XXVII

Monday 28 April

My dear Betty,

Mr. Johnson and Mr. Harrison have been dining with me, and I sit down to answer your letter to night, being engaged to write a long Paper to the Surveyor General Tomorrow. I must first rejoice with you upon the good Prospect our dear Children face of getting well through their present Distemper which I assure you has given me great Anxiety. With respect to the Post-Chaise, I beg of you to act according to your own wishes. If the Carriage be exactly as you approve of I should rather recommend it to you to purchase it. What I mean is, I would not have you to have the lower prized [sic] one if the other is more eligible. The best and most fashionable one will in the End be the cheapest. You had better get your Friend at Bishop Auckland to view them for you. Will he be willing to take our Chair at a fair Price? What shall I say more to you about the Island? The fated order is come from the Treasury to the S.G. to make an offer of it first to us and if we decline to Mr. Worsop.[102] Mr. Harrison advises me to send a Remonstrance to

---

[101] Loyal Duncan first began to run between London and Sheffield in 1797, then later to Leeds by Barnsley and Wakefield.

[102] The terms were that if, after adjustments and allowances, their offer exceeded Worsop's, at that time the highest bidder, the lease should be made to them, otherwise to him. In his report to the Treasury of 1 March, the Surveyor General argued that as the present lessees could begin to embank the outmarshes immediately they were assured of the lease, the work could be completed by 1801, whereas a new lessee would not be able to begin until after the expiry of the lease in 1802.

the S.G. and I have contrived to do it[103] but really I don't expect much good from it, as they seem determined to make the utmost Advantage of it. A Letter is come to Day from James Pinkerton, professing himself to be in Partnership with Mr. Worsop etc. and offering to advance in their Bidding if necessary. Mrs. Foss seems averse to joining us,[104] if we exceed Whitlock's Valuation: but Outwith and the other Parties wish me to secure the Renewal at any Rate. I have told Mr. Harrison I was determined to do it, if no better Terms can be obtained. I shall present my last Remonstrance in the Morning. But when the final Answer will be given is uncertain. So that you must get our Chapel taken Care of as well as you can. If you can get the Like Duty so much the better. With respect to the Sacrament Day, I think Mr. Sanderson might be obtained. But if you can hear of a curate entirely at Liberty you had better engage him if you can have him in future. I told Mr. Harrison your great Desire of retaining the Island, if it was not intolerably dear. And he recommended me to try another Application to the S.G. and Mr. Pitt. It cannot take above a week or ten Days longer, at least I heartily wish it may be so but there is no saying positively.

The Moment I am at Liberty, I will not lose a Day in coming to you. I had absolutely determined to come on Thursday next and went to the Revenue Office this morning to announce my Intention but Mr. Harrison strongly pressed me to try another Application to which I have unwillingly assented, tho' I believe as I said before, it will do no good. I have lately had very bad Nights from my great Anxiety about the End of this Business. You must not blame me for you would have felt the same. I will come again to the Carriage. If it is such a one as you wish to have, it must [illegible] and you can enter it when you please: and to wait 2 or 3 years longer would be tedious especially if you think it will be productive of Health. That is the greatest Blessing and cannot be bought too

This together with the lessees' acceptance of Whitelock's valuation and their offer to advance themselves the money required for the improvements made their offer the most attractive before Worsop's intervention on the last day for applications and the Surveyor General had recommended its acceptance in his draft report of 22 February. The rents which he had suggested as appropriate for the lease were £403.16.6d. for the first year, £1,687.9s. for the second, and for the remainder £3,254.9s. per annum or £3,000 if the Treasury agreed.

[103] This is letter XXVIII.

[104] She later sold her share to the other lessees for an annuity. See Letter IX, n. 57.

dear. In short, believe me most sincere in saying that I will never oppose anything which is for your real Happiness. If you determine to have it let Jo. look out for a Horse to match the young one, or if you please, I will enquire here, but perhaps you would not want one till the autumn. I dined with Mrs. Harvey yesterday, who entertained me most hospitably. She has received her Parcel from Mrs. Mountjoy safely. I am sure I paid Dawson for the will, and daresay the other Bill was paid before. You must examine your Books. You must take care about your [illegible], on account of poor Meggit's Death. Would you have me go to see Jack, before I leave Town? Perhaps it would do no good but only unsettle him and it has but an odd Appearance to have stayed so long in Town. I think I might write to Mr. Blenkinsop. With respect to the Income, my Notion is, that we should endeavour to give in no more than we can afford to pay afterwards and if 40£ would satisfy them, it really seems as much as we can afford to pay. Would it be right for you to give it in yourself or to wait for my Arrival. I shall take your Advice about coming in the Mail. What time does it reach the Dax. I am just returned from presenting my letter to the S.G. There is nothing but Treachery. Mr. Harrison shewed me a Letter from Mr. Whitelock very much in our favor but never shown to the Board.

J.L.

XXVIII
[*To the Surveyor General*]

April 30th 1799

Sir,

I have received Mr. Harrison's letter of the 26th inst enclosing a copy of the Resolution of the Treasury on the several offers made for a part of the Sunk Island Estate; and it is with extreme concern I observe that the present Lessees are allowed only the option of having a new Lease upon coming up to the *highest* offer of the other Applicants, with the Abatement of 5 per cent upon the value of the Rents offered by them, and the repayment of the Expenses incurred in defending at Law the Rights of the Crown.

I observe that it is declared in the Minutes Of the Treasury of the 4th of November 1794, printed in the Appendix to your first Report to Parliament, Page 93, "but that the Lessees of the Crown sho: d have a Deduction of 5 per cent from the Nett value as *ascertained by Surveyors* in the manner prescribed in the Act of the proceeding Session of Parliament".

If the allowance of 5 per cent directed by their Lordships Resolution to be made in our Case had been really a Deduction from the nett value ascertained by the Land Surveyor for the Crown and who has sworn to his valuation in the manner prescribed by the Act, we sho'd have rec'd it with great Thankfulness, and have acceded without a murmur to the Terms offered to Us. But it is with great disappointment I observe, that they are only a Deduction from the extravagant offers of Adventurers and Speculators, who seem to have no other object in view but that of wresting this Estate out of the Hands of the old Lessees, by whose Family it has not been barely improved, but as it were created for the Crown.

As the Resolution of their Lordships seems to be founded on an Idea that the Embankment of the Island had been a Speculation of great Profit to the Undertakers, I will beg leave to state, that so far from having been profitable for the first seventy years it appears by Affidavits sworn in the year 1757, that Mr. Wm Gylby a Barrister at Law, and who had been in possession of the Island for above 50 years, declared a short time before his death, that his Fortune had suffered severely by improving it, and by the frequent Inundations, and other Accidents attending it. We were far indeed from expecting an improper degree of favor on Account of these Circumstances. Our Confidence only was, that they would not be entirely overlooked, and that we should at least not be treated worse than other tenants of the Crown. But we are compelled to lament that after you had made us the offers, contained in "the outlines for a Proposal for granting a new Lease from the Crown",[105] you should have thought yourself obliged to secede from the offers so made to Us, and to receive offers from any other Persons, and that their Lordships should have allowed themselves to deprive us of the advantages held out to us in that Communication, without any other Alternatives than whether to accept Terms, which we have Reason to believe would be hazardous or to reject at once all the Prospect of being benefitted by the long and unremitted Exertions of our Ancestors.

I have taken no little Pains to inform myself during my long

[105] i.e. those of 5 May 1798. See Introduction pp. 31-2.

Residence in Town upon the Applications what has been the practice of granting Crown Leases since the passing of that Act, and
cannot find there has been any Example of a Bidding of this kind
for a Lease against the Lessees of the Crown; but that the general
Practice has been to prepare Terms to the Lessees, and not to admit
of offers from other Persons, until those terms had been refused:
And let me still indulge the Hope, that the Lessees of Sunk Island
will not be treated by Government with unexampled and unmerited
Severity, in being made the only Instance of a Departure from the
general Rules established in favor of the Tenants of the Crown after
having so much Reason to expect from the peculiar Circumstances
of their Case a more than ordinary degree of Mildness and liberality
in the Terms of their Renewal.

We therefore humbly but most earnestly entreat you to have the
goodness to reconsider this subject to represent their Circumstances
to the Lords of the Treasury, and endeavour to prevail on them to
alter the Deduction of 5 per cent, ordered by their late Resolution
to be made from the nett value ascertained on Oath by their own
Surveyor, whose deservedly high Character both for Probity and
Professional Judgement can leave no room to doubt the Truth or
accuracy of his Calculations.

May I be permitted to add that if you will have the goodness to
recommend this to their Lordships to grant us a new Lease upon
such terms as we may safely accept, we trust that the Anxiety you
have manifested for the Advancement of the Land Revenue of the
Crown will be gratified in seeing this Island improved to its greatest
Capacity, as we are determined to commence the necessary Works
for that purpose the Inst:ᵗ their Lordships final Resolution shall be
communicated to Us, and are very anxious for a speedy determination, that another Season may not be lost.

I am with great Respect, Sir

Your most obedient servant,

J. Lonsdale

XXIX

Saturday Afternoon
[May 4]

My dear B.

As soon as I received yours of this Morning I immediately posted to the Revenue Office and begged an Audience of the S.G., and which I obtained with Difficulty as he said he had nothing to communicate to me. The Apprehension suggested by you of Mr. Harrison's possible Insincerity made me importunate in requesting to see him. He said my last letter to him was in the Hands of Mr. Pitt and that he would press him to determine upon it immediately and that he would send to me without delay his ultimatum. He owned the Arguments I had made use of were very just, but pretended to say Mr. Pitt was afraid of establishing a bad Precedent. I ventured to tell him the Badness of The Precedent would be entirely on the other Side and that we should be the first Instance of old lessees having been treated with such severity. Nothing more can now be said or done. The whole matter lies between the S.G. and Mr. Pitt. All the rest are mere Cyphers. As soon then as I receive this ultimatum I have made my mind entirely up to accept it.[106] We are to pay immediately in the commencement of the new Lease what we had agreed at the end of eight years, 3200£. I have used every Caution with Respect to Outwith, having got his own letters, as well as Declaration to Mr. Marris. He is very eager to have the Lease obtained and will join me, if all the Rest refuse. Mrs. Foss will not join us, if we exceed Whitelocks Terms, and says she will give up her share to me, if I will allow her a small Annuity. She adds, thro' Mr. Marris, that she is more likely to die in 3 months than to hold out 3 years.[107] What Answer do you think I have given to this kind offer? If we give up the Island at the end of our present Term, we are to receive from Government 1000£. I have ventured to tell her then, that if she gives up to me her Share, I will pay to her Portion of that sum. Is this behaving like a Coward in this Business? Your idea of giving in our Lease to government is out of the Question. They want to receive, not to pay any Advance. But I must stop my pen with this Assurance that you will

[106] In fact he did not wait. See next Letter.
[107] See Letter IX, n. 57.

not have more Pleasure in hearing, than I in communicating to you the Conclusion of this very unfortunate Business.

I will take your Advice in returning by Bawtry by way of securing the ground. Will the Roads be good enough for the chair? I shall have my new Hat in a Box; but it might be taken out there, and carried perhaps on Horseback. I think you seem to incline to my not buying a Trunk. Do you really wish me to purchase any Prints, and of what sort? And with Respect to Cheeses, what do I do? The Expence of painting a Carriage [illegible] The silver cyphers are now not much in use, but the plain cypher on the Rim just below the Window on coach side. You don't tell me how you hope to get the Prayers at the Chapel on the Sacrament Day supplied. Is my Hint about Sanderson likely to be practicable? Mr. Bingley, who you say is going into orders seems worth enquiring after. Would an Application to Mr. Johnson be the most proper means of doing it? or by way of meeting the present Necessity it might not be amiss to enquire about Mr. Simson's usher. Happy shall I feel myself if I can supercede the use of both of them. I am, thank god, very well and I shall endeavour to keep myself so by great Care and Regularity. It may seem stupid in me, but I never go out in an Evening and get to Bed about 10 o'Clock. What a precious time for musing is Bed! You don't mention poor Jack. Have you heard nothing more about him. I have been thinking perpetually about writing to Mr. Blenkinsop or Mr. Briggs but the Possibility of being gone before I received their Answer has hitherto prevented me. Add to this the unpleasantness of explaining so long a Confinement in Town. Mrs. Coore's Family go to the Montem and promise to see John. If my Paper would suffer me, I could not stop writing on.

J. Lonsdale

P.S. I rejoice with you upon the hopeful situation of the poor children. Do not expose them too much.

XXX

London May 8th 1799

[This letter to the Surveyor General
is in Lonsdale's handwriting though
signed by him and Johnson]
Sir,

In Mr. Lonsdale's letter of the 30th of last month he took the
liberty of laying before you some observations on the Resolution
of the Lords of the Treasury communicated to us by the Copy of
Mr. Long's letter of the 24th of April, relative to the Renewal of the
lease of the Sunk Island Estate, in the hope, that their Lordships
would upon your Representation of the Case of the Lessees be induced to moderate the Terms on which they had directed a new
Lease to be offered to us: And we felt ourselves very much indebted
to you for the Information You were pleased to give to Mr.
Lonsdale, that you had submitted to Mr. Pitt some fresh Proposi-
tions in our Favour.[108]

We shall assuredly receive with proper Thankfulness any Relaxa-
tions from the severity of the Terms proposed by their Lordship's
Resolution, in which no Consideration seems to have been had of
the Expences incurred by our Ancestors in the Embankment of this
Island from a bare Sand, nor any Allowance made for the large
sum of £8,940 now to be laid out in the further Improvement of it,
yet the anxiety we feel to bring this long Protracted Business to a
Conclusion induces us to trouble you with another Letter; without
waiting for an Answer to the former, to signify to You, "that even
if their Lordships should not be induced to make any Statement
in the Terms offer'd to us, we have resolved to accede to those

---

[108] The Surveyor General wrote to Long 9 May. "When you told me Mr. Pitt had
considered the proposal I made that a further Term of two years should be added
to the present lease of Sunk Island as compensation for the loss which the lessees
had incurred prior to 1755 and for the defense of Crown rights since that time and
that he had determined not to agree to that proposal I assured you that I should
give neither him nor you further trouble on the subject having done all for the
lessees whose Case I think to be a very hard one that seemed consistent with my
duty. On my return I found a letter from them of which I send a copy enclosed
from which you will observe that notwithstanding their Apprehension that the Rent
may prove to be more than the Estate is worth, they have determined to run the
risk of taking it on the terms proposed by the Treasury rather than to part with a
property that has been so long possessed by their ancestors."

Terms, in the firmest Confidence, that if upon a fair Trial they sh.^{d} be found to be too hard for the lessees their Lordships will at some future Period grant them such Relief, as the Circumstances of their lease shall be found in the justice to require.

From Mr. Harrison's statement of the Substance of their Lordship's Proposal we learn, that the terms offer'd by Mr. Worsop after making the Deductions allowed in favor of the Lessees are as follows:

> Net Rent for the first Year   £621 : 11 : 0
> For the second Year   £2088 : 10 : 0
> And for the Rem.^{r} of the Term £3188 : 10 : 0

But as it seems to be required by their Lordship's letter, that the offer of the lessees, including their Deductions sh.^{d} *exceed* that of Mr. Worsop's, we beg Leave to propose the following Rents.

> For the first Year   £630
> For the second Year   £2090
> And for the Rem.^{r} of the Lease £3190

But at the same time we cannot but hope that the Facts stated in Mr. Lonsdale's letter before referred to will meet with due Consideration from their Lordships, & Yourself and that the very unprecedented case of the Lessees of Sunk Island will be found to entitle them to milder Terms than those of the highest Bidder among so great a Number of Persons, entire *Strangers* to the Estate, who have become their Competitors on this Occasion: And we mean only, that this Letter sh.^{d} be considered on the Part of the Lessees as expressive of their Resolution not to decline the new Lease on the Terms offered in the Letter of Mr. Long, if more favorable ones cannot be obtained.

> We are with the greatest Respect
> Your most obed.^{t} Servants
> J. Lonsdale
> Alex.^{r} Johnson.

XXXI

My dear Betty

I have had a very unpleasant Foreboding for the last 2 or 3 days that all was not well with you: and truly sorry as I am to find my Fears confirmed. For Heaven's Sake, if not for my Sake, take care of yourself, for nothing else can damp the Pleasure I feel in coming home to you but the Apprehension of finding you unwell. Thank god for the poor children being well again: John too is "perfectly well and perfectly happy" to make use of the very words of Mr. Blenkinsop. With Respect to my going to the Montem it was absolutely impracticable, every Bed having been engaged at least a month before. But, as I told you before, I shall have an Account of him from Mrs. Coore and it is not prudent to teaze and trouble the Tutors too much.

I will now return to that wearisome subject the Island, but surely no one has more Right to call it so than myself. If I have erred on any side, it has been in thinking too constantly and deeply about it. And thus, I have argued with myself. If the Island can be retained so as to yield us decent Interest for our money perhaps it would be wrong to give it up for ever. And I think from my own Reassurings and from the best information I can get from Outwith that it cannot pay us less than ten p. cent. for our money expended. That is, if the Embankment etc. can be done for 8000 £ we must receive at least from it 800 £ p. ann. There will be full 4000 Acres, and if according to your supposition they will be worth 20s. p. Acre, there will then be a 1000 A left for ourselves. The Rent will be 3000 and odd pounds not quite 3200; And the Repairs will all fall upon us. These are surely hard Terms, and what I would not engage in but from the Hope of a future Advantage to my Children and which may be considered for a kind of perpetuity. What do you think I have done since my Acceptance of them? I have forced myself to call upon Mr. Smythe. He seemed astonished at our accepting them, as he thought them too high, but he said they cannot reject the highest Bidder. I took my leave of him with this Request that he lend us all the Assistance in his Power. Will you not allow me some Credit for doing this? I gave in my Acceptance on these Conditions, that we hoped still to receive some more mitigation and that we trusted not to be used worse from our great Desire not to lett go an Estate so long enjoyed by the Family. To place your mind still more at ease, we shall be at Liberty for 2/3 or 3/4 months, to consider about this Business and the Treasury will be bound by their own Warrant. You have surely given me time enough for the Execution of my Business. As soon as I hear from Marris and Outwith I hope matters will be soon finally settled. To show you I have not been entirely inattentive to your Requests, I have bought you a Box of Lunn's Pills: and a Couple of Prints. The Subjects are the Birth of our Saviour and his Celebration of the Last Supper. They are a guinea each and therefore I did not chuse to buy any more without further orders. The present rage is transparent prints, placed in windows. They are very beautiful and would become the Central Square of our Bow very well. What is the size of it? And would you like to go to such expence? We shall not now begin our Works on the Island till Spring and If your Brother could then supply us with money it would prevent our selling out to Disadvantage. Perhaps a 1000£ would serve our Purpose as the Funds may advance before that time. I hope now I shall have no more occasion to trouble you upon this Subject till things are absolutely settled. If they form any more objections, it must be on the Score of covenants and Security. I have shewn my new Transfers to Harrison for the sake of deriving all the Consequence I can. If Mrs. Foss does not sell me her share, she must join in Responsibility. Your Account of poor Whitenose's bad eyes is very unwelcome to me. I should think a Dose or two of Physick, as he can be spared from his work, would be the likeliest means of restoring him. Let Jo. ask Dixon and Ben North's advice, and if they think proper, by no means neglect it. I am so pleased with the servants behaving well to you, as to feel an inclination to bring them some little Reward home with me. What if I bring a cambric Handkerchief for Betty and an handsome Ribbon for Mary? Tell me the Price I should go to or what else would be more proper. Your letter is again charged double, from the Paper being so thick and chargeable. This is the Chamberlain's message to you. Nothing at present can afford greater satisfaction to me than a better Account of yourself.

(This letter lacks a signature)

XXXII

[23 May]
Thursday Afternoon

My dear Betty

I have barely time to answer your Letter, but, as you say you will expect a Letter on Saturday, am unwilling to disappoint you.

I am happy in learning your Cold is leaving you, I beg you will endeavour to guard against a Relapse. You may put a Period to all your Arguments about the Commencement of our Lease etc. Things are so very slippery, that I have determined to have it immediately and as well conditioned as it can be obtained. You will not wonder at this, when I tell you, that this very morning I was informed a first Bidding was made of £150 p. Ann. more. I hastened down to the Revenue Office, I was sorry to find my Letter of Acceptance had not yet been formally signified to the Treasury.[109] I entreated Mr. Harrison himself to go to present it, and he says there can be no Doubt of the bargain on both sides being valid. I mention this to show you what ticklish ground we stand on and that there is no ground for nice Disquisition. Mr. Harrison observed to me to-Day, that unpleasant as my long Confinement here may have been, we certainly could not have obtained our Renewal without it. Our opponents have now bid 400 £ p. Ann. more than we are to have it for: so that if they are Judges, our Bargain is not a bad one. But this is not a convincing Argument to me, as there is such a thing as bidding from Ignorance, Passion and Opposition. We must make the Experiment. Mr. Harrison thinks I may be able to return home towards the end of next week but I will write to you again on Monday or Tuesday. I will endeavour to execute your Commission for you.

After returning from the Revenue Office I made my call at Mr.

[109] The acceptance had been communicated informally (Letter XXX, n. 108). The Surveyor General made a formal report to the Treasury of the lessees' acceptance of their terms on 14 May, forwarding with it copies of Lonsdale's last two letters to him (XXVIII and XXX). In his report, the Surveyor General sets out Worsop's and the lessees' offers exactly as in Letter XXX, and adds of the latter "These I conclude will be accepted by your Lordships". The new lease was to be in the names of Lonsdale and Outwith in trust for themselves and others. The caution he had suggested in his former report was advised because some of the numerous applicants "seem not to have the means themselves of laying out the sum of £8,490 estimated to be necessary for the further improvements. Mr. Lonsdale and Mr. Outwith cannot however be justly considered in the light of speculators. I am well informed they are possessed of property exceeding £20,000".

Milnes', was most graciously received and invited to dine on Sunday. Mr. and Mrs. Richard Milnes[110] are with them and the Dixons. I am sure you will think I am sadly out of my [missing] There will be no use in Marris coming now as the only Security we can have now is a warrant from the Treasury, that a Lease shall be granted to us in the Course of 2 or 3 months, and which to us will be a sufficient Security. What do you think I have heard this morning but that Col. and Mrs. Kearney are in Town. I will wait upon them Tomorrow or next Day, if Business does not prevent me. I think you said you could provide for the Sunday after Trinity. Pray who is it by and what Notice will be necessary, if I should be enabled to come from next week? I don't now see any evident necessity of returning by Bawtry as there will be time enough afterwards for settling our Business about the Embankment etc. Yours most affectionately J.L.

XXXIII

June 6

My dear Betty

Your Behaviour has been so affectionate, steady and patient during the tedious Prosecution of the present Business, that I always feel the most sensible Pain when I cannot write to you what I know you wish to hear. But what, for God's Sake, should Mr. Dixon know of the Prudence of a Bargain except he understand the terms of it. And how he would get access to Mr. Pitt is above my Comprehension except he had something to communicate to him interesting to government. I have called upon Mr. Rennie[111] twice without

---

[110] Richard Slater Milnes, 1759-1803, of Wakefield and Fryston, took over Houghton Hall, Darfield but only lived there 10 months and then moved to Fryston. Married Rachel Rodes of Darfield. M.P. for York city 1784. Died in London in house of James Milnes.

[111] John Rennie, 1761-1821, eminent civil and mechanical engineer, and friend of William Pitt. After working as a millwright, in 1784 he went south and worked for James Watt, assisting him in the design of the steam engine. Later he carried out canal construction and for many years was connected with extensive drainage operations in the Lincolnshire fens. He built several bridges and designed London Bridge which was completed by his son, Sir John Rennie 1794-1874. Two features characteristic of Rennie according to C. T. G. Boucher, *John Rennie 1761-1821* (Manchester University Press, Manchester, 1963) appear here, his plain and forthright manner and his integrity. "He scorned to obtain work by submitting low estimates, leaving his employers to face a swollen bill, when the actual work was executed" (*op. cit.* 23).

being able to obtain much Intelligence from him. The first time he was going to attend the House of Lords and the next not at home. I have left a Note for him to fix his Time. He seems to be a shrewd sensible Scotch man, and not very communicative. I really don't know, as I said before, how far to engage him, or what Fee to offer him for his Advice. He seems to rate the Expence of Embankment as high as old Pinkerton, and upon this degree of expence will depend the Wisdom or Imprudence of renewing our Lease. I have a letter from Mr. Marris this morning to say, that Mr. Outwith, Mr. Welch, Mrs. Horton etc. will be all ready to join me in giving any Security to Gov: they may desire. Mrs. Foss only refuses "and as I did not accept of her offer about purchasing her Share, does not feel disposed to make me another offer".[112] Mr. Marris prefers me to come by Bawtry. What do you think of my doing so?

Before I wrote any further, judging of your own unease by my own, I determined to go down to the Revenue Office and solicit an Audience of the S.G. whom I have never had the Honor of seeing since our Acceptance of the Terms of the Lease. He was engaged with Company, but received me with great good Nature and advised me to write a Letter immediately to the Treasury, under his Name and Recommendation, soliciting their Lordships to come to an immediate Determination of this Business. I accordingly sat down in the Office to do it and Mr. Harrison has engaged to deliver it himself this morning to Charles Long Esq. their Agent and Secretary. If the Security expected be only a reasonable one for the faithful Performance of our Bargain I will sign it, but if it involves anything dangerous to you and my children, you may depend upon my not consenting to it. I will sooner follow your Advice and give up the Island. The S.G. said very slowly "I have mentioned the Dispatch of this Point several times to your Aquaintance Mr. John Smythe". Mr. Pitt, he says, is really so much engaged with public Business as not to be got to anything else. I hinted applying to Mr. Pitt myself. I will now then at last come to the Income, about which I find I am extremely confused. You are not according to my Conception obliged to state from whence that Income arises. And you may very honestly make large Deductions from the Island on account of Expences about Renewal, and present Repairing of Banks, etc. What I mean is, I should not like to give more in this year, than I should hold to the next. Is not both the Chapel and

---

[112] See Letter IX, n. 57.

Darfield over rated? I would certainly call the Curate 60 or 70 as
he may be said to assist at both Places. After all this, I wish to do
right, and beg of you to send me exactly what I am to copy in my
next Letter, with Directions how it is to be sent, expressed and
signed. I wish you may not think my Faculties impaired by the
thick atmosphere of London. Having spent so much money, I get
to be very covetous; and I could like excessively for you to be able
to purchase the Chaise you mention to me. I have 50£ yet in
Bolland's Hands which surely will more than bring me back to you.
I am as careful as I possibly can. I have bought for you, however,
¼ lb of rhubarb and a Paper of Ching's Worm Powder which is
said here to be the best Physic for Children, exclusive of worms. I
have enquired too for a Paper-Case, which to have it handsome will
cost 17ˢ. Would you have me buy it? You have put me to the
Necessity of ordering a new Wig by your talking about my waiting
on Mr. Pitt, for really my old one is become very shabby.

If you don't hear from Eton soon, would you have me go there?
Mr. Kearney left an Invitation for me to dine on Saturday. I fear
there is another Party; as it prevents confidential conversation. I
think it might be good Policy for you to answer Stubbing's Letter
civilly, saying I have a very good opinion of his judgement and I
shall be obliged to him for his Advice. You may say I am detained
longer in Town by the Crigglestone Inclosure Bill. It may prevent
at least his being an Enemy. Tell Joe to be careful to get good
Turnip Seed. I think there is some in the House. He must endeavour to sow with the Appearance of Rain. If the Horse has no
Physic perhaps Grass would do him good, as soon as he can be
spared. Can you truly call me an idle correspondent.

Yours J. Lonsdale

If Lodges' Horse would suit one of the children perhaps our brown
Horse might suit him for the Cart

XXXIV

Saturday 2 o'clock
[June 15]

My dear Betty

It is a great consolation to me to find that you and the children
continue tolerably well; for really I can say nothing more for myself,

having been for the last week much affected by the very slow and uncertain Progress of my Business; Mr. Harrison being now out of Town on Affairs relating to the Land Revenue. I determined therefore to pursue a bold game with them. I waited again upon Mr. Smythe on Wednesday, told him I was willing to Sign a Bond for 10,000 £ for executing the promised works[113] if they continued to insist upon it, and that if that would not satisfy them, I was determined to give up the Application. I then sent a Letter[114] to the S.G. expressive of the Same Resolution and referring him on my *own* account to the 5200 £ invested in the Funds. This very morning I have been waiting on him to receive his Answer and am most happy in telling you it is quite as favorable as could be expected. It is this "In consequence of your Letter, I have had a long Conversation with Mr. Long (not saying a Word about Mr. Pitt, Mr. Smythe etc) have pressed with him the very long and unjustifiable Delay you have suffered and have prevailed upon him to despatch your warrant immediately, I hope today". The Condition only is, that if our Works are not done during our present existing Lease, we must then give Security for the Performance of it.[115] All this is, I think, very fair and I made no Hesitation to assent to it. You say, I ought surely to be the best Judge about taking the Lease at the same time express your Desire of having it upon any promising Terms. In answer to this I must remind you, that I gave you my own opinion on this Subject in a former Letter, as far as I could form it from my own Calculation and Mr. Outwith's Representations and that the whole depends greatly on the Sum to be expended in the Embankments etc. before the Land can be profitable. Thus far however, as I told you before, I have made up my mind, that it is certainly politic to take the Warrant for a new Lease and which, contrary to your Apprehensions, we have undoubtedly a Right to dispose of; if we dare not make the Experiment ourselves. I will, if possible, get the Lease made to myself and Outwith only; and then we shall have a proper Check upon the other Lessees who may be unwilling or unable to join us in the Expence, and the Danger. I have invited a Mr. Rennie a third time but find he has been out of Town, ever since my Note was left for him. If he returns in time for me, I have

---

[113] A bond for this amount was entered into by the lessees.

[114] This letter has not been located.

[115] The Treasury required the lessees to bind themselves in the sum of £5,000 in case they had not expended the £10,000 in the three years after 1 July, 1799.

requested to be immediately acquainted with it. I will now proceed to give you a Proof that I have not been inattentive to your repeated mention of a Carriage, tho' I have not said much to you about it. I have found out in Holborn a very likely one, built in London about 4 years ago with its second wheels almost new, painted a good dark brown, and wanting only fresh varnishing which would cost 2 guineas and the Arms taking out and your own Cypher inserting. It belongs to a Mrs. Stacey near Sheffield and has not been [used] since the new Taxes. It was brought here [missing] by her son. She is a Relation to Col. Ather[ton of] Sheffield. Now if you feel a Desire to purchase it, would it be best to apply to Mrs. Stacey herself about it: or to be content with having it examined here. There is only a Boot and Box under the Seat. The Coachmaker says he would send it to Ferrybridge by some of the Lawyers in their approaching Circuit. What do you say to all this. If we could afford it *now*, you may always depend upon my Disposition to oblige you. The Price is 30 guineas. It seems to be a light one, but hung high enough for the present Fashion but this, he says, might be remedied. I always neglected mentioning our own Chair to you. If it is meant to be used, the Rims of the wheels want examining. Remind Joe of this and talk to him about it. With Respect to Joe I need only say that I am willing to give him 12^s and the usual Cloaths if he is weary of keeping a sheep but it is unreasonable to ask both. He should give you an answer immediately as I very lately met with an old steady Servant out of Place, who can have a very good character. You say not a Word how my Duty is to be done and yet you must see how entirely uncertain now my Coming is. The drawing of the Warrant, if no *new* obstacles occur, will take 3 or 4 days, passing thro many Hands. I hope I shall have now time to write to Outwith about the Welches and if I could return by Eton and Birmingham, it would certainly be best. You should give me more Directions about the Doyleys. Take care of yourself and Children.

J.L.

P.S. If your Potatoes are of a good sort Joe could not be better employed than in getting as many as we are likely to need.

XXXV

Thursday Noon
[June 20]

My dear Betty

If you love me, I am sure you must pity me. When I last wrote to you, I felt the warmest hopes of seeing you soon. The Prospect now, as I told you might possibly be the case, is not so promising. I saw Mr. Harrison on Monday and was congratulated by him on the probably speedy Issue of my Business. He requested me to visit again next Day, and attended me to the Treasury to enquire for the Warrant. To our great surprise and mortification we found it not made out, and Mr. Long demurring, whether it could be done without another Board of the Treasury being held. Upon our Return to the Revenue Office Mr. Harrison assured me that Mr. Fordyce was highly offended, and promised to complain of it immediately to the Lords. Not, however content with this, I have made an Application Today to a Mr. Hammond under Secretary to the Ministry and who I am told will be the most likely Person to persuade Mr. Long to dispatch the Business. Mr. Pitt is out of Town, indisposed with a Cold. It appears now very plainly, that an opposition is, and has been carrying on against us in the Treasury, independent of the Surveyor Gen: There is no Doubt however, I hope, but he will carry it thro' in our Favor, and Mr. Harrison goes so far as to say, I may come safely down into the Country and leave it to them. Mr. Johnson however advises me to the contrary, saying that I must not by any means desert it. I am extremely dispirited and exhausted with these so frequent Delays but will try and comfort myself with the Hope, that my next Letter may assure you all is done. I agree with you in opinion "that if we can but raise the money for the works and the country flourishes, there will be no Doubt but the Island will answer in the End." I feel myself very much indebted to Mr. Wood for his very friendly Behaviour to us: but should be sorry to have you to press upon him too far. With Respect to the Income, I really think in my Conscience you have given it in high enough. There is one Article in your Calculation which I am sure ought to be omitted and that is the House and Fees at Darfield which belong to the Curate by the Curate Act, as an Appendage to his Salary. And this being taken off would leave the Tenth exactly 60£ Whatever you may think, it will not be a pleasant thing to withdraw the Rents from the Island the next year, nor am I sure it will be legally right. I never like to begin higher than I can hold out. If there be a Statement called for, be so good as send a form of it for me to copy and sign. I will now touch a pleasanter string to you. I went very early this morning to thank Mrs. Kearney for an Irish gown she sent for you and to wish them a good Journey to Walton on Saturday. Mr. K. asked me very handsomely to take John there in my leaving home, but I think this would not answer, except you come up to Town and stay here till the Vacation commences, and go [missing] with me. What a [missing] pleasant thing this be! I had never before an opportunity of talking gravely to them. I embraced the moment of mentioning your Wish for his being a Trustee to our children, which he acceded to in a very friendly manner. I told him as I felt, that I should not last much longer, if my Business was not done. Notwithstanding; what you said about my not buying for you the Chaise I mentioned, I have sent a man employed in the Coach Business to look etc. He is a Person Mr. Hardcastle lodges with and whom he described to me as a good Judge. What fee will he expect for his trouble? I want your advice perpetually, I find myself a poor Creature without you. What I meant about the Repairs of our own Chair only was, to get the Plate round the wheels so secured, as to be fit for a Day's Journey or two.

You may tell Joe that I think certainly the Lambs will pay best to be sold, as soon as they are fat, that he must not lose the first opportunity of a good Price. I have no objection to keep the handsome one he mentions. As to the wool, if Mr. Wood's man will give me a good Market Price, I shall prefer him to any other Person. Only remind Joe to be very exact about weighing it. Tho Kemp or the Milnes will assist him in doing it. I still think I was right about Joe's Wages. He should not have them both in money and sheep pasture. If however his Boots will not serve him the third year, I am willing to make up the Deficiency on account of his good Behaviour to you. I wish the Blister may prove of service to you, and if you think a little Physic proper, you should by no means defer it till the warm weather comes on. The Nights here are become very hot and troublesome to me. I think from your Account Thorpe Arch might suit Harry. Mr. Kearney is an Advocate for Trade in preference to the Army. Mrs. K. wonders you should send Mary to school. All is military here. Nothing but glittering Arms and nodding Plumes.

J.L.

XXXVI

22nd June

My dear Betty

By yesterday's Post I received a Letter from Mr. Marris and another from Welch, wondering very justly at the long Delay of our Business and lamenting that so fine a Season for our Works should be lost. The substance of these I laid before the S.G. this morning and he really seems to sympathize with us in the very hard usage we have met with. But both he and Mr. Harrison absolutely decline applying any more to the Treasury about the Warrant, having already subjected themselves to improper Treatment on that Account. The S.G. recommends it to me to call again upon Mr. Smythe and Mr. Long and after that, if no Execution can be obtained, he thinks I may safely return into the Country and begin our Works, not seeing any possible Danger, which can arise from it. As soon as the Warrant is sent to him, he will order the Lease to be made to Mr. Outwith and myself in Trust for the other Parties. Mr. Johnson will take Care to send down the Lease to us, and perhaps everything will be done as well as if I were in Town myself. I will take Care to get a proper Clause inserted in the Lease, as a security to us from the other Parties, and which I will leave in the Hands of Mr. Harrison for that Purpose. I have been just writing to Mr. Marris to this effect and if he or Mr. Outwith approve of it, you may perhaps see me at Newmillerdam on Saturday next. But I will write to you again on Tuesday or Wednesday as soon as I receive Mr. Marris' answer and if I am obliged to come by Bawtry will tell you about sending the Chair for me. This will make it necessary for you to send to Wakefield on Friday Night, if you don't receive my Letter on the Thursday to enable me to set off early on Saturday morning. But all this, you see, depends upon what turns out on Monday and Tuesday; and on Mr. Marris' Answers. You are sure it is very mortifying to me not to bring our Business to full Conclusion: but you will not, I suppose, chuse me to remain here 3 or 4 weeks longer, i.e. till Parliament breaks up. With Respect to myself I am entirely resolved to do, as shall appear for the best, and wish you to speak your real sentiments about the present Plan. With Respect to returning by Eton, tho' it would certainly have given me great Pleasure, yet I don't see what real use it would be etc. as a Letter to Mr. Blenkinsop and Mr. Briggs may answer as good a Purpose for they have no time or Inclination to spend in private conversation.

[This letter is not signed]

XXXVII

Tuesday Afternoon
[June 25]

My dear Betty

I was much disappointed in not hearing from you on Monday and really worked myself up into a Belief that you was not well. Happy am I in having my Fears so well removed. I have a Letter too from Mr. Marris begging and entreating me not to leave Town, without seeing the Warrant for a new Lease. I waited upon Mr. Smythe yesterday and I think he would not see me. I left word however by his Servant that I would call again To Day. I have been admitted and have pressed the matter to him in the strongest Terms. He hopes the Business will be settled in a few Days without troubling Mr. Pitt who is too busy to be spoken to: but he still thinks himself that Security ought to be given as our opponents were to have done so. In Short, I have not a Doubt that himself and Mr. Long have all along been against us. He begins now (and which I was glad to hear) to claim a merit in assisting us. This Idea I was glad to encourage and must beg of you to be very cautious in saying nothing to the contrary. Sorry am I to find the great Pains I have taken to explain everything to you so much thrown away. Do you believe the idle suspicions of your Neighbours more than the faithfull and repeated Assertions of your Husband. The Terms offered to us by the Treasury were never rejected but only endeavoured to be softened and were finally and unconditionally, acceded to so long ago as May 8th. The Attempt made to overbid us was subsequent to it, and could have had no bad effect but that of Delay. The S.G. has always been very steady about this: so much so as to give me Leave to return home, and begin our works. And with Respect to Mr. Harrison, he has been so much our Friend, as to expose himself to Mr. Long's Resentment by his Solicitation for the

Execution of the Warrant. Mr. Smythe told me to-day that he had behaved very impertinently and that Mr. Long had been obliged to forbid him his office, a plain Proof to me that Mr. Smythe and Long are connected. I have dwelt so tediously on this Subject to convince you, that we are sure of having the Lease on the First Terms proposed and if it cannot be obtained without signing a Bond, Mr. Outwith will join me in doing it. And to prove to you I am not asleep about the Business, I went yesterday to dine with Lawyer Wood, to consult him about the most proper Article for securing ourselves against the other Lessees. Mr. Hammond too the Under-Secretary of State will apply to Mr. Long for me, after which I will wait upon him myself if Mr. Smythe does not keep his Promise with me; but he advises me to wait quietly for a few Days longer, before I importune them any more. Our attempting to give a Bribe to Mr. Long who is a Member of the House, and a Creature of Mr. Pitt's, might undo our whole Business. Don't listen to such ignorant Insinuations! Have I said enough to you? Tired to Death as I am with Fruitless Application and tiring my Acquaintance with the Sight of me yet willing to hold out a week or two longer if you wish it, I must beg of you to speak out and assure me that you would be happy in my doing it. Without this, I am determined to seek Refuge in coming home to my poor Children. Notwithstanding my saying all this, I am quite as well as can be expected, except my resting badly in the warm Nights. With Respect to the Duty, why cannot you apply to Mr. Lodge, who would do it as well and reasonably as any Body. As I told you before, the other Parties, who confine me here, must join in the Expense. As to the Income you have given, I think still it is quite enough. If you find from Mr. Wood, that it can be paid here, I am very willing to do it. Mr. Carr of Wakefield who is here, says it is too late for my doing it. If you will follow my Advice about John, leave everything to Mr. Blenkinsop, to whom I gave orders to furnish him with everything really proper and fit for him. Every Body here complains of their great Extravagance. As to poor Henry, I am willing to indulge you in your own opinion. My only partiality for Thorpe-Arch was its healthy situation. I think my offer to Joe is a very fair one. If his Boots only last two years, I will pay for them. Let him give you an Answer. I hate to be imposed upon. Believe me to remain, tho' a Prisoner, yet truly and affectionately yrs. J.L.

XXXVIII
[*To the Surveyor General*]

London June 28th 1799

Sir,

Agreeably to your Direction I have waited again upon Mr.
Smythe, who assured me he had conferred with You and Mr. Long
upon the Subject of our Warrant: "that he hoped everything w^d
very soon be despatched. Hearing however nothing from the
Treasury, I am under the unpleasant Necessity of troubling you
again for your Advice and Assistance.

If you think the Warrant for our new Lease will soon be issued
I sh^d certainly be sorry, after so long a Continuance in Town for the
Sake of giving more Satisfaction to my Co-Lessees, to return into
the Country without it. But if you suppose a considerable Delay
may still be likely to take Place I w^d then beg Leave to entreat you
to have the Goodness to grant us your Licence to commence a Pre-
paration for our proposed Works immediately. For tho' the present
Season be too far advanced for entering now upon the Embankment, yet a Beginning may be made for the operation of the
ensuing Spring by making Bricks, and providing other necessary
Materials.

I desire to offer my grateful Acknowledgement of your very
polite Attention to me, during this tedious Application, and to assure
you, that I shall always remain,

Your most obliged humble Servt

J. Lonsdale

XXXIX

Saturday Noon
[29 June]

My dear Betty

I am just returned from Mr Bollands who took me to Guildhall
and has very obligingly requested a Mr. Curtis,[116] member for

---

[116] Sir William Curtis 1752-1829. He and his brother inherited a family business
in sea biscuits at Wapping. He was also successful in the Greenland fisheries and as
a banker. He was an Alderman of the Tower ward 1785, Sheriff 1789, Lord Mayor
of London 1795-6. Elected M.P. for the city in 1790, he held the seat for 28 years.

the City, to speak to Mr. Long in my Favor, and in the Afternoon I am engaged to take my Tea with Mrs. Thirkhill, when I hope to meet with a Mr. Lodge, my Intercessor with Mr. Hammond the Secretary. But all this I believe, will be of very little Avail, the People in the Treasury being such Lords Paramount, as to set at Defiance all sollicitations. They are generally behind Hand in their official Business, 8 or 10 months. I mentioned Mr. Marris' Letter to you urging me, if possible, to obtain the warrant before my Return; but since, I have got another from Mr. Welch, in the name of Mr. Outwith, recommending it to me, if much longer Delay is likely to take Place, to obtain the Surveyor Generals Permission in Writing to begin the Works. I therefore wrote a Letter to him yesterday to this Purpose with the Advice and Approbation of Mr. Harrison.[117] Indeed Mr. Harrison is clearly of opinion, that we had better have done this a month ago, as it would have helped to remove the necessity of Security being given, and as the Treasury cannot recede from the Bargain sufficiently agreed to by Both Parties. I will however go to Mr Smythe again on Monday and if possible get the Contract brought to its regular Conclusion. Unluckily for us, the S.G. has taken offence at Mr. Long's Behaviour to Mr. Harrison and is determined, as he expresses it himself, to "wash his Hands of the Business". You will say what I *feel*, that this is a most Shocking Account! Your Friend Johnson is so tired out, that he will not budge a single foot to serve me: His Ward Steer has run away from his military Academy and I met him yesterday swearing and cursing like a Bow-street runner in Pursuit of him. Who, he says, would wish to have children?

Your Civility to Miss Zouch[118] is very well applied and I wish you to continue it. Her uncle Zouch has been the best Friend I have in the World. I cannot surely feel any Objection to your plan for visiting the Sea. There is nothing I more ardently wish for than the Recovery of your Health. And your Sister Ann will be both a pleasant and an useful Companion to you, in case of Indisposition. I entirely agree with you that poor Mary will be better with you, than in Miss Hemingway's School. And if you should want

---

He supported Pitt and the war and was created a baronet for steady voting in 1802. Though a very poor speaker and ridiculed by the Whigs, he was a man of great importance as head of the Tory party in the city (*Dictionary of National Biography*).
[117] i.e. Letter XXXVIII.
[118] Niece of the Rev. Thomas Zouch. See Letter XV, n. 77.

my old Favourite Betty the Cook, I will bring her to you. I think you must be mistaken in saying that Jack will not leave School till the middle of August as I understand it to be the last week of July. Do you make any point of my returning by Eton? If you do, I will certainly do it, tho' I feel an unpleasantness in doing it from *this* place, having so long a string of Reasons to give to account for it. With Respect to the Duty, manage as well as you can, for I don't know how to direct you. You don't explain to me what Armer said improperly. Joe's Behaviour appears to me to be too obstinate: but for your Sake, I am willing to submit to it. Settle it as well as you can, either by finding ourselves a pair of new Boots every two years, or, if that will not agree with his Pride, by expecting him to do so. My Reason for saying this is, that perhaps he may take our money, and make his Boots last for three years. I will write no more till I can send you a better Account. Write as often as you can yourself. It is time to set off to Mrs. Thirkill's

Yours truly

J.L.

P.S. It just occurs to me that the Sea Terrace at Burlington[119] was broke into last winter. Perhaps it has been repaired. The Place we visited near Scarbro, I am told, is much improved in Accommodation.

XL

Wednesday, July 3rd '99

My dear Betty, (Mr. Bingley's Dog is a thing promised for many years: I don't know I want one, but if I can find quarters for it without troubling you, do as you please: I am very easy about it.)

I by no means wonder, that your Spirits and Temper are quite worn out by our very tedious correspondence. But, believe me, the unpleasant Acc[oun]t in my last letter was not at all exaggerated. The Revenue Office and the Treasury quarrelling among themselves, and we very likely to be Sufferers by it. I thought it right therefore to catch Hold of every Chance of Assistance that presented itself. Both Mr. Curtis and Mr. Hammond used all their Interest with Mr. Long; but, I believe, to very little Purpose. Sheltered under the Favor of Mr. Pitt, he is insolent and intractable to the

[119] i.e. Bridlington.

last Degree. I stuck therefore closely to Mr. Smythe, I have thrice waited upon him, since I last wrote to you. He leaves London on Monday next, and was obliged therefore to assist me: or declare to the contrary. On my attending upon him yesterday and as I told him for the last time, he desired me to meet him at the Treasury at 2 o'clock when our Business was concluded by himself and Mr. Long and a Minute made for our Warrant being sent to the Treasury.[120] It was read to me by the principal Clerk for my Approbation; but I found there was no Room for making any objections to it. We are to give a Security of 5000 £ for the Completion of our Works if they are not finished during our present existing Lease. So slow are all their operations that the Warrant will not reach the Revenue Office till Tomorrow or Friday: but after that Mr. Harrison promises to release me as soon as he can, So that, I hope you may depend upon my taking care of my own Chapel on Sunday Sennight. If I find I have time to stop at Bawtry, I will send for the Chair to meet me there: if not, I will push directly home to you. I have been writing this morning to Mr. Marris and to Mr. Welch to this Purpose. Perhaps you will not be quite weary if I trouble you with another Letter on Monday or Tuesday but I think you must not write to me later than Saturday or Sunday if you find any occasion for it. If my better wig be not at home, you may as well send for it from Wood's, as a Stranger should be decent. Having now a good many things to bring, a Packing Box will be necessary, and how will this come home in the Chair? Consider about this; indeed about everything. In spite of my great gayety I have not yet been at Vauxhall nor seen a Play since poor Jack left me except one with the Kearneys. My going to Ranelagh[121] was entirely a matter of Accident, and in some respects unlucky as I appeared there in my old Coat among a very splended company.

---

[120] Treasury Minute July, 1709 (P.R.O. CRES/2/1446). "The Solicitor General has communicated to the lessees of Sunk Island the Treasury resolution for the renewal of the lease ... the new lease is to be made out to the Rev. J. Lonsdale of New-millerdam and to Humphrey Outwith in trust for themselves and the several other persons interested in the present subsisting lease according to their respective shares".

[121] Vauxhall and Ranelagh were the two most outstanding examples of the 18th century love of distractions and shows of all kinds. Vauxhall, whose grounds extended for about 12 acres, came into being at the time of the Restoration and continued until 1859. Ranelagh was situated in part of the grounds of the Chelsea Hospital of to-day. Concerts, which usually ended at 10 p.m., were held in the famous rotunda, but the company often stayed until midnight when there were fireworks.

A Gentleman dining in the same Box offered me a Ticket, being disappointed in his Company, saying [the] fireworks would be very fine. I came away as they were over, about 12 o'clock. Did not you charge me not to look dull and dreaming? in the streets? Let me however whisper one Truth in your ears: I have often looked cheerful with a heavy Heart.

My Reason for not going to Eton sooner were from my Desire of returning that way, and exploring the Road. If I find myself at Liberty towards the End of the Week, I will still go over. The love of *him* your dear son, lies close to my Heart. With respect to your proposed jaunt to the Sea, I think, as I said before, your going with your sister a very good opportunity; for, as you hint to me, it would not be very decent for me to leave Home, the moment I am come to it. If you can send a civil message to Hardcastle or any of others, it may save the trouble of a Letter. Mrs. Thirkill has been a Treasure to me: She is almost blind: but her mind is enlightened. I have bought you some Doyleys and two transparent pictures for yourself or Mrs. Zouch,[122] as you shall determine. I don't know clearly what kind of a Pocket Book you want. Your account of dear Mary's being well and merry is musick to my Soul. I entirely agree with Mrs. Kearney in opinion that it is a Pity to confine so young a girl to a School. Will you believe, I tremble upon reading what I have said about coming home: so many mishaps have attended it.

Yrs
J. Lonsdale

XLI

Tuesday, 9 July

My dear Betty

(The school at Eton breaks up July 29th and begins Sept. 1st)

Too true are your Fears that the Warrant will not be executed for my returning home to you this week. I have been in the Revenue Office and the Treasury, almost every Day since my last, and without effect. This very morning I received a Letter from Mr. Harrison, informing me that that Draft was at last received and wishing to see me. After sitting two Hours and settling at Intervals the Pre-

---

[122] Wife of the Rev. Thomas Zouch of Sandal.

liminary of the Lease (for really the Number of Callers at the Office are innumerable) I was told to my great Mortification, that the warrant when indorsed was still to be signed by 3 of the Lords and could not be done at the *soonest* before Thursday and not sent to me before Friday morning. I ask you now to say candidly what would you have had me done? I received a letter from Mr. Marris this morning advising me by all means to see the *whole* Business done: And you say, "pray don't leave Town, till you get the Warrant and all completed". In answer therefore to Mr. Harrison's assuring me that I might safely come without them, I have determined not to do it but to quit Town the moment I am in Possession of them, and to come directly to Newmillerdam. For Mr. Marris says in his Letter, that after Thursday, the day appointed, he is going out of town for a few days, but would meet me at Doncaster some Day next week. But if they are not willing to meet me at Elmsall Inn, I may as well go on to Bawtry and stay all Night. What will you now do about the Duty? I think you had better send immediately to Hemsworth and entreat Mr. Vollans to spare him. If you cannot get him, I would even venture upon Lodge for once. You have been so very troublesome to your Neighbours Would not even Mr. Rogers be obtained for the Morning? The Reflection upon the Difficulty you will be under is very distressing to me. Has Mr. Braithwaite never written to you? Let me hasten to a pleasanter subject. Unwilling as I was to show myself again from this Place and not seeing the Advantage of it in as good a Light as you seemed to do, yet always happy in the Power of giving you Pleasure I went to Eton on Saturday last. And how glad I am to send you a good Account of your dear Boy. He appears to be much grown, and is very well. I waited upon both Dr. Heath and Mr. Briggs who join in speaking of him with great Respect. If you feel as suddenly as I did, a tear of Joy will mount into your Eye. He breaks up in three weeks from yesterday and I propose his coming thro' London to Mr. Joseph Bolland's[123] in Cheapside and to be put by him into the Duncan coach. Dr. Heath mentioned Mr. Smythe's son being to come down by the same road. The other Boys would not answer. With respect to your journey to the Sea, I wish you to do what is best for your own Health. If you can leave me at home, it may be

---

[123] Mr. Joseph Bolland, 1760-1827, son of John Bolland of Masham. He is buried in Masham churchyard and an inscription records that, after 40 years engaged in the City of London, he retired to his native land for the rest of his life.

more convenient and saving. But if my Duty can be taken care of, and it is at all essential to your Enjoyment, you know I am Devoted to your Service. If you can go with Ann to Scarbro', why will it not suit you as well as Burlington. In hopes of seeing you the Beginning of the week.

Yours
J.L.

XLII

Monday Afternoon
[15 July ?]

My dear Betty

As soon as I had read your Letter this morning, I determined immediately to come home to you. The Trouble you have about the Duty is intolerable. Besides, I see clearly, that if I defer my Return later, there will be an end of your Sea Journey, which after so long a Confinement and so patiently endured, you certainly have not a Right to be exposed to [illegible]. Mr. Harrison invited me to dine with him yesterday, being the only Day he is at Liberty and really his Behaviour to me was entirely open and friendly. The Warrant, he says, is already signed by two Lords of the Treasury and wants only a third signature: but such is their Indolence, that he cannot promise me, when he will obtain it. It is however of no consequence and when it is obtained, he will immediately send a Copy of it down to me. There is no Fear of our having a new Lease upon the Terms agreed to. The great Point is, whether the Terms acceded to are so good as we ought to have been entitled to. And in this Respect I may be of more use at Home than here, by examining closely into the Merits of the Case. I will take Care to leave everything upon safe ground, and I have not a Doubt of the S.G.'s being sincerely a Friend to us, however offended he may be, and I think justly, with the Treasury. I am just returned from taking a Place in the Duncan Coach for myself on Thursday next and for John Lonsdale on Tuesday July 30. Mr. Jos. Bolland will meet him at the Windsor Stage on Monday evening and in the morning put him safely into the Duncan. He is an extremely good-tempered steady man, without children and Miss Bolland[124] who

[124] Margaret Bolland 1751-1823. Only daughter of John Bolland of Masham. Died in Masham unmarried.

is now with them says I may safely give the same good character of Mrs. Bolland, a very grave and affectionate woman.

Tell Joe to spare no Expence in putting the Hay into [illegible], and into every secure state, as I am much affraid the weather is likely to be very ticklish. If anything happens to the contrary of what I have written I will contradict it on Wednesday Night, but at present I hope to see you on Friday, and am in haste to save the Post

Yours most affectionately
J. Lonsdale

XLIII
[to Harrison]

Newmillerdam,
7th November –99.

Dear Sir,

It has not been pleasant to me to observe so long a Silence, but the very rainy Season and late Harvest cut off all Hope of doing anything on Sunk Island with Effect: Besides I wished to follow your Advice of consulting first Mr Rennie or Mr. Jessup,[125] but who unluckily happened Both of them to be engaged. Mr Jessup was in London, and at the Isle of Portland, and Mr Rennie did not come to his Works at Grimsby and Boston,[126] till the Beginning of October. On the 16th however I met him at Hull, and attended him to the Island; whom he examined the Outmarshes with great Attention, and marked out the precise Dimensions of every part of the Embankment. He settled also the Contract for us,[127] and Sett

[125] William Jessop c.1750-1814, civil engineer, pupil of Smeaton, and chiefly connected with dock and canal construction, including the West India Docks, the Grand Junction and Caledonian canals. Smiles (*Lives of the engineers*, II 198, n.) describes him as "the first engineer who was employed to lay out and construct railroads as a branch of his profession". To him is attributed the replacement of the flanged tramway and flat rimmed wheel by the flanged wheel and flat edged rail.

[126] Rennie was consulting engineer for the improvement of Grimsby Haven 1797-1800, a scheme involving the diversion of the River Freshney and the construction of a dock and entrance lock. He submitted two designs and estimates for a new bridge over the Witham at Boston in 1800.

[127] Another characteristic vignette of Rennie—"He never trusted to any assistant, he designed everything to the minutest particular with his own hand, specified the manner in which it was to be made and specified the price. He directed in the same manner every design whether of bridge, road, canal, dock, drainage, or

the Work to Persons formerly employed by him at Grimsby. A beginning was made October 25th, but if the present very bad Weather sh^d continue, I fear it must retard their Progress.

I have discharged Mr Whitelock's Bill, and shall be glad to remit the Money to you for the Lease fee, as soon as I am favoured with the Amount of it. I need not remind You to make the proper Insertions for our Security the Contract for the Expences having been signed only by Mr. Outwith, and Myself; and wch we cannot enforce upon the other Lessees, till the Leases is obtained.

I entreat you to present my respectful comp[limen]ts to the Surveyor General and to assure him, that the Engagement we have entered into shall be executed with Fidelity.

Be assured that I shall ever retain a grateful Sense of the great Attention and Civility shown to me by the Surveyor General and yourself, during my long Residence in Town, and that I am truly,

Your obliged humble Servant

J. Lonsdale

XLIV
[to Harrison]

Newmillerdam,
January 13th, 1800

Dear Sir,

Tho' I have not yet been favoured with an Answer to my Letter of the 6th of Novr. yet I sh^d not have troubled you so soon again but at the earnest Importunity of Mr. Outwith.

We have had upwards of 200 men constantly employed in the Embankment, and there is now a great Prospect of having it finished, and the Outmarshes fit for Cultivation at Lady Day: So that you see we shall be ready to grant Leases to Others, before we have completed our own.[128] One Half of the Money has been ad-

harbour. It was in the first instance sketched out by himself, then the mode of construction was specified, then estimated and then the general report explaining the whole was writen by him. Clerks then merely copied." (Ms "Life of Rennie" by his son Sir John Rennie and cited by Boucher, *op. cit.*, p. 21).

[128] *The Hull Advertiser and Exchange Gazette* for 18 January 1800 had an announcement: "Eleven capital farms to let of rich warpland in Sunk Island the greatest part of which is now embanking, . . . suitable farm houses with convenient outbuildings . . . a chapel and a wind cornmill are intended to be erected." The farms were to be between 300 and 500 acres and the tenancies to run from Ladyday (25 March) next.

vanced by Mr. Outwith; so that he may be excused for feeling some
Anxiety about the Business. And with Respect to Myself too perhaps
I ought to inform you, that I have at last thro' Mr. Marris's Inter-
ference purchased Mrs. Foss's Share; and for wch I am to pay her by
an Annuity for her Life.[129] I will depend then upon your Goodness
in submitting this State of the Business to the Surveyor General,
and in requesting his Permission to have the Lease executed, as
soon as may be convenient to you.

My little Boy from Eton is now with me, and reminds me to
thank you for your very friendly Attention to him. You will be glad
to hear, that I have a very good Acc[oun]t of him from his Tutor.
His Verses have been sent up, as they express it, for good: and he
has obtained from Dr. Heath an Advancement in his Term. Pray
have you Batchelors any Idea of the Feelings of a Father on such
occasions?

I will not detain you any longer but only Beg of you to present
my respectful Comp[limen]ts to the Surveyor General, to whom,
as well as to yourself, I most sincerely wish many happy Returns
of the present Season.

I am,

Dear Sir,

Your very humble obed^t Servant,

J. Lonsdale

XLV
[to Harrison]

Newmillerdam,
February 1st 1800

Dear Sir,

Having received no answer to my two last Letters addressed to
you at the Revenue Office, and not having yet forgot the unhappy
Miscarriage of a former one, I am tempted again to trouble you at
the particular Request of the old Tenants, who are now soliciting the
Retaking of their Farms, and are anxious to know the Conditions of
our new Lease.

Mr. Whitelock is now here as a Commissioner for our own
Enclosure;[130] and you are sure I could not help consulting him upon

---

[129] See Letter IX, n. 57.
[130] At Crigglestone. See Introduction p. 8.

this Subject: He gives me Room to hope, that we shall not be restrained in plowing the new Land, only laying it down again to Grass in a proper Proportion at the Close of our Term. An Assurance however of this will be an Encouragement to the Applicants, and enable us to make steady Agreements with them.

I am but just returned from Sunk Island, where our Embankment is going on very successfully; and I have now no Doubt, if we escape any Misfortune, that the Land will be ready for Cultivation at Lady Day. I need not tell you, that the late Short Days and bad Weather have obliged us to increase our Wages considerably. As the Price of Timber is now so exorbitantly high, Mr. Outwith, my very active Colleague, hopes it w$^{d.}$ not be a very unreasonable Favor to ask of Government to have our Bricks made on the Island exempt from Duty: He desires me to say to you, that it w$^{d.}$ be an Encouragement to us to increase the Number of Farm Houses, and that he thinks six instead of three w$^{d.}$ not be too many. It is our Intention at present to erect a Wind Mill[131] for the Accommodation of the Tenants.

You will pardon me for requesting the Favour of an immediate Answer to this Application; and I trust you think too well of me to make it necessary for me to add, that I have not forgot your long and continued service to me.

I am, dear Sir, with Truth

Your most affct. hble.Servt.

J. Lonsdale.

PS

If our Lease sh$^{d.}$ happen to be in Readiness I have a Friend now in Town, whom I w$^{d.}$ entrust safely with the Care of it. You will oblige me by presenting my respectful Comp$^{ts.}$ to the Surveyor General.

---

[131] Though an advertisement announcing this intention to build a windmill appeared in *The Hull Advertiser and Exchange Gazette* for 18 January 1800 (Letter XLIV, n. 128) and though there is a calculation of the number of bricks required at the end of Letter XLVI, it is doubtful whether it was ever built. It is not included in the improvements credited to the lessees in the new lease of 1804 nor is it shown in any maps of about this time.

XLVI
[to Harrison]

Newmillerdam
Feb. 24th 1800

Dear Sir,

I have received your very friendly and obliging Letter[132] with great pleasure, and rejoice to hear the Heads of our new Lease are already prepared and that we may hope very soon to have a Draft of them. Nor can I entertain the least Doubt of their being such as we shall approve: The new Land must of course be plowed for it's [sic] necessary Cultivation and Improvement, and with Respect to the old we shall willingly submit to such Restrictions, as may appear proper for the real Good of the Estate.

I have consulted our Superintendent about the Bricks likely to be wanted on the Island and am quite astonished at the Number he has given in. When you read the Account, and add to it the Expence of an Embankment, Subdivision of Fences, the Making of Roads &c.: &c:, I think you will readily believe the 10,000£ with w$^{ch.}$ Mr. Smythe saddled our Warrant, to be very soon exhausted.

I shall be glad to learn the Surveyor General's Idea about the Addition of Cottage Houses. Does he mean to annex any Portion of Land to them? If he will favour us with his Direction they shall with Pleasure be attended to.

Two of the principal old Tenants have agreed to retake their Farms, with a suitable Proportion of new Land laid to them. Mr. Stubbing,[133] to whom I made a Point of offering his Farm, has declined it; having, as I am told, another very eligible one in his view.

There is a general Apprehension, as we always foresaw, of the new Land not being productive for the first two or three years. We have determined therefore, and I am sure you will think equitably, to make Ourselves responsible for such bad Consequences, and to

[132] No copy of this letter has been found.
[133] See Letters VIII, n. 53., IX, n. 56. *The Hull Advertiser and Exchange Gazette* of 18 March, 1800, announced a "Sale of stock off Stubbing's and Roper's farm, cattle, implements and upwards of 1,500 sheep and a large quantity of hay to be carted off the premises".

receive Rent in Proportion to the Success of the Experiment.

I have now only to entreat you to pardon my repeated Importunity, and to believe me to remain with great truth,

Dear Sir,
Your most obliged and obed.t Serv.t
J. Lonsdale.

"A Calculation of Bricks wanted for Sunk Island"

5 new Farm Houses at 150000 each	=	750000
2 Cloughs		100000
Augmentation & Repairs of old Buildings		400000
4 Cottages		80000
Chapel		90000
Mill		60000
Bridges		40000
		1520000

I rest entirely upon your Friendship in promoting the Dispatch of this Business as much as is in your Power, and if Mr. Outwith's and my own Attendance in London shall be necessary, to acquaint us with it.

XLVII
[*to Harrison*]
Dear Sir,

Mr. Jackson the Bearer being suddenly called to Town on Business of his own, I have only just time to tell you, that he is Son in Law to Mr. Outwith, and a very worthy Man. If you can make him an Instrument for the Execution of our Lease You will do us an essential Service.

If my own and Mr. Outwith's Attendance in London can be dispens'd with, it is certainly most desirable; but we shall submit with Pleasure to the Opinion of the Surveyor General.

I am with the most real Respect
Your affectionate humble Servant,
J. Lonsdale.

Hull 4th June [1800]

XLVIII
[*to Harrison*]

Newmillerdam
May 8th 1801

Dear Sir,

I am at last happy in hearing from you and which I have long and impatiently expected.

In my Answer to your Letter of 25th Nov. in w$^{ch.}$[134] you observed to me that there was now no Reason why our new Lease should not be proceeded in, I mentioned Mr. Jackson's Proposal of sending an Affidavit of our Disbursements:[135] My Intention was to have prevented it, if you had disapproved of it, but he says he understood from you in London, that it was a proper and necessary Step. He has certainly kept below the Sums we shall have to expend, the making of the Roads and other heavy Articles not being included. So expensive is building now become from the Price of timber, that I paid the other Day 500£ for only two Barns, w$^{ch.}$ have been added to two of the old Farm Houses.

An Application to the Board of Treasury for an Alteration of the Terms of the Warrant is what I had never any Idea of; having always considered them as fixed and determinate, by w$^{ch.}$ we were to stand or fall. All I looked forward to was that the Surveyor General in his own Department might be induced to befriend us, in Proportion to the Spirit of our Improvements.

The very kind Interest you are pleased to take in my Affairs, and your warm Wishes that the Island may ultimately prove Advantageous to me deserve my most grateful Acknowledgement. And I am happy in saying to you, that if we continue to escape Misfortunes, and the Times remain favorable to Agriculture, things I hope may turn out very well. But I dare not talk so boldly as your Hull correspondent seems disposed to do. There are many things ag[ain]$^{st.}$ us w$^{ch.}$ they do not attend to.

The Embankment being so extended, and more exposed to the Sea than the old one, will be a great and constant expence to us. The Want of Water too is a terrible Defect, and must lessen the

---

[134] Neither Harrison's letter nor Lonsdale's answer have been found.

[135] Jackson's affidavit, dated 12 March 1801, certified an expenditure of £14,968 since 18 November 1799 (P.R.O. CRES/2/1444).

Value of the Land, if we cannot in some Degree remove it. This we are preparing to do by sinking Wells, and making Cisterns for holding Rain Water to every House. So that you will easily see that our Rental at present cannot be ascertained, being engaged to a Diminution of such Rent in Proportion to the new Land proving unproductive, and wch. in many Parts is likely to be the Case. The Money also laid out by the Tenants in levelling and filling up Creeks has been very great and must be accounted for by us, if the crops sh^d. not answer to them.

Our Agreement for letting the Land is for 21 years. No old Land to be plowed up, and one Third of the New to be laid down to Grass at the end of 7 years. These Conditions indeed were mentioned to you at the Time, and you did not make any Objection to them.

Agreably to your Advice we have allotted 7A: of Land apiece to 6 or 7 Cottages, and about 20A: each to a Carpenter, Miller, Blacksmith, and Superintendent; and most of the Houses are already built.

But I shall weary you with this tedious Detail of Particulars and will now conclude with repeating my usual Request to you, that you will proceed to the Dispatch of our Lease as soon as you conveniently can. I have indeed lately been more anxious than ordinary on this Head, having been confined to the House for the last six weeks by a very bad sore Throat, and wch. kept perpetually returning upon me. I am now, thank God, getting better, and hope soon to be stout again; but I am sure you will feel for me, how unpleasant even the Apprehension must have been of leaving my Affairs in so unsettled a state.

I will write then to Mr. Jackson not to teaze you any more with his Agents, and shall hope for the Favor of another Letter from you very soon. I have heard nothing more from Mr. Topham Secretary to the Sons of the Clergy, who promised to settle the Rent in Dispute in an Amicable Manner.[136] The last year's Rent was p[ai]^d. to the Tenant, and there is another now nearly due. If any more Obstruction happens I will acquaint the S.G. with it. I beg my respectful Comp[limen]^ts to Him and am your obliged and obed^t: Servant.

J. Lonsdale

[136] Ombler, the Sons of the Clergy tenant, had refused to accept the payment offered by the lessees for the use of the road. See Introduction pp. 26-7.

XLIX
[to Harrison]

Newmillerdam
June 8th 1801

Dear Sir,

I know enough of your great good Nature to believe that you would not so long have denied me the satisfaction of an Acknowledgement of my last letter, if the constant succession of Business you are engaged in had not prevented you. My Situation at present is this. Mr. Outwith is perpetually importuning me to attend him and Mr. Jackson to London: and I continue to assure him, that everything is going on there properly under your Direction relative to our new Lease without the Necessity of such Attendance: but at the same time you may be well assured, that for the Reasons assigned to you in my last I w^d not by any Means neglect the most effectual Means for the completion of this Business.

I omitted mentioning to you before, and w$^{ch.}$ I hope there was not much occasion for, that if any Money is wanted to be laid out in the Process of this Application thro' the different Offices, a Draft shall immediately be sent to you from the Wakefield or Hull Bank.

I am just returned from Sunk Island, where we are very busy in improving and enlarging the old Farm Houses. We propose adding a new Barn, Stable, and Granary to each of them; and the Hall House is to be entirely new gutted and rebuilt. We are also laying Cliff Stone[137] on the Road leading to the Island, w$^{ch.}$ we hope will entirely obviate any objection made to us by the Gov$^{ns.}$ of the Sons of the Clergy. A Plan and Estimate are got for the Chapel, and w$^{ch.}$ we find cannot be done for less than 5 or 600£; but cannot at present be proceeded in from the Want of Bricks for the above mentioned Purpose, and w$^{ch.}$ we are now getting made as expeditiously as possible.

I most warmly entreat the Favor of a Letter from you
and am very truly,
Your obliged and Obed$^{t.}$ Servant
J. Lonsdale

[137] Chalk from quarries at Hessle Cliff, by the Humber four miles west of Hull. Whitelock (Report p. 144) calls it Whitecliff stone.

L
[to Harrison]

Dear Sir,
  It is really painful to me to be so very importunate in my Application to you; but having received no Answer to my two former Letters, I am strongly tempted to trouble you again. Mr. Outwith is now with me at Sunk Island, and we are very anxious about compleating our Leases with the Tenants. I will only repeat to You, that we shall be glad to remit a Draft for any Sum You are pleased to order for the Discharge of the Expences of the Lease; and that you may depend upon your own great and long Services to me not being forgotten. I hope to be at home in a few Days, and shall wait impatiently for the Pleasure of hearing from You.
                    I am, dear Sir,
                        Yrs. most truly
                          J. Lonsdale.
Sunk Island
7th July 1801

LI
[to Harrison]

Dear Sir,
  Seeing in the Paper yesterday the Marriage of William Harrison Esq. of Tavistock Street, Bedford Square, I cannot help concluding it to be your own. I beg of you therefore to accept my most sincere Congratulations and best Wishes for all the Happiness of that State. Your Mind having been so agreably occupied has I hope been the sole Cause of my not hearing from you. Ever since I had the Pleasure of knowing you, it has been my constant Endeavour to deserve your Esteem; and I am wholly unconscious of having done any thing to forfeit it: I will still hope then at convenient opportunity to have the Pleasure of hearing from you—With Respect to Sunk Island, I can add nothing to what I have said in my former Letters. If our Application for the Completion of the Lease shᵈ· appear premature on Acc[oun]ᵗ of the Chapel not being yet

erected, it shall immediately be set about, the only Causes of Delay having been the Want of Bricks, and if indeed we had purchased them, the Tenants having been too much engaged to lead them. You may safely assure the Surveyor General that I am determined to execute every Part of our Engagement with the Strictest Fidelity.

Mrs. Lonsdale joins me in best Comp[limen]^{ts} to Mrs. Harrison, and I am

Yrs. most truly
J. Lonsdale

Newmillerdam,
18th August 1801

LII
[*to Harrison*]

Newmillerdam,
Dec. 29th 1801

Dear Sir,

In my letter of the 21st last; after stating, as you had desired, the Particulars of the new Building and other Improvements made by Myself and my Co-Lessees on the Sunk Island Estate, (on wch. we have expended already no less than £16,887,4—and must necessarily expend as much more as will make the whole Expense at least 20,000£, tho' the Estimate for those Works did not exceed £10,000) I ventured to express my hopes that the Exertions we had made and sh^{d.} continue to make for the Improvement of the Island would sufficiently plead with the Surveyor General for every reasonable Indulgence in his Power to grant us.

Not knowing what Indulgence the Surveyor General might be able to show us, and being extremely unwilling to ask anything that could be deemed improper, I felt myself at a loss to make any specific Request; but as the Completion of our Lease has been deferred nearly three years (probably for the better enforcing the Conditions of our Contract) and as we have not only in that Interval amply fulfilled our Undertaking, but have incurred an Expence of nearly double the Amount of the original Estimate, we hope it will not be thought unreasonable on our part to request that these three years may be added to our Lease, by making the Term up to 31 years from this time; which I presume would have been done of Course, (and more especially in favor of an Undertaking of this expensive and hazardous Nature) if our Application for a new Lease had been delayed 'till the expiration of the old one.[138]

I beg the Favor of you to lay this Request before the Surveyor General, and am

Dear Sir,

Your most obliged and very humble Servant

J. Lonsdale

LIII
[to Harrison]

Newmillerdam
March 27th 1802

Dear Sir,

In your last very obliging Communication you promised to write to me again very soon, and to request the Surveyor General to settle the Covenants of our new Lease. Will you have the Goodness to pardon my impatience in reminding you of this Promise and begging the Favor of a single Line from you. My Reason for thus importuning you is an Intention of going to Sunk Island in a Week or ten Days, where of course, I shall be teazed by the Tenants about fixing the time for signing their own Lease. I suppose you know, that I was honoured with a very handsome Letter from the Treasury, acquainting me with the Order given for our new Warrant. It will give me Pleasure to hear you have got the necessary Signatures to it, and that everything is going on well. I need not I hope repeat to you, that any necessary Remittance during the Progress of our Lease shall be always ready, when called for. I shall be very thankful for an early Answer, I am with most sincere Respect

Your very h[um]ble Servant

J. Lonsdale

[138] Harrison replied on 15 February 1802, that he had seen Mr. Smythe, a report had been before the Board and orders had been given for the issue of a warrant for the extra three years.

LIV
[to Harrison]

Newmillerdam
July 21st 1802

Dear Sir,

I did not return any Answer to your last very kind Letter in March last,[139] because I am always unwilling to give you unnecessary Trouble, and because you said you hoped very soon to be able to communicate to us the Covenants of our Lease. But the Business of Parliament being now over, and the Surveyor General probably leaving Town, I am tempted again to sollicit your Attention to our Interests. And I am particularly requested by my Co-Lessees to mention to you, that our Rents from Sunk Island being received in January and July, they wish the Rental to Government to be paid at the same times.

I trust in your Goodness to me to pardon this my repeated Importunity, being convinced I am confident in your own Mind, how much I wish for a Conclusion of this Business. The Favor of a Letter[140] from you at your Leisure will be very acceptable to
Your most obliged h[um]ble Serv.ᵗ
J. Lonsdale

LV
[to Harrison]

Newmillerdam
Feb. 18th 1803

Dear Sir,

After so long a Silence I almost hope you will compliment me on my Patience in not having troubled you any sooner. I rested with Confidence in the Assurance given to me in your very obliging

[139] Harrison had written on 31 March that the Treasury warrant for the lease had received the necessary signatures and had been sent to the Land Revenue Office; that the Surveyor General had prepared a memorial to the Treasury on the subject of the covenants to be included in Crown leases in general and that those to be put in the Sunk Island lease would be regulated by the orders made in consequence of the Memorial, and he hoped to be able before long to communicate them to Lonsdale.

[140] Harrison replied 27 July (see next letter). The Surveyor General had now gone into the country after an unsuccessful attempt to obtain from the Treasury an answer to his memorial about covenants. As some consolation he enclosed a copy of the Treasury warrant extending the lease for three years.

Letter of July 27th, that the Completion of our Lease was delayed solely by the Want of an Answer from the Treasury to the Surveyor General's Memorial on the Subject of the Covenants of the Crown Lands in general: And I now only write again to you at the pressing Sollicitation of my Co-Lessees, who you must suppose on many Accounts to be naturally very anxious for the Dispatch of this so long depending Business.

Our new Chapel is at last finished, after many repeated Delays in our Builder; and you will not be surprized to hear, that the expence greatly exceeds his Estimate, from the Addition of Chapel Wall Stable etc: wch were found necessary for the Accommodation of the Tenants. As soon as the Weather and Roads will permit, I propose going to open it, and to appoint a regular Minister to the Clergy of it. I am glad to be able to add, that it is a very elegant little Building.

I took the Liberty some time ago of requesting you to consult the Surveyor General about our Road to Sunk Island and think you gave it as his Opinion that the original Consideration of five Guineas p$^{d.}$ annually for the Use of it sh^d not be departed from. The Tenants are particularly careful not to commit any Trespass or Injury; and we have lately made a separate Road for the Delivery of their Corn, so as not to interfere with or infringe on the Road belonging to the Sons of the Clergy. Their Tenant however Mr. Ombler still refuses to accept the customary Acknowledgement and threatens to renew his Complaint to Mr. Topham Secretary to the Sons of the Clergy. I have prevailed on him to defer doing it, 'till I receive from you final Directions how we are to act in the Matter. The only bad Part of the Road falls upon Ourselves to repair, and wch we are willing to do so that I cannot really see any just Cause of Complaint. I rec$^d.$ a Letter in the Beginning of this Business from Mr. Topham upon the Subject, who seems to be a liberal [minded] Man, and to wish only that no Encroachments may be made upon the Estate.[141]

I shall hope for the Favor of your Answer to this Letter, as soon as shall be convenient to you; and am, with my respectful Comp[limen]$^{ts.}$ to the Surveyor General,

Dear Sir,
Your very sincere Servant
J. Lonsdale

[141] See Letter XLVIII n. 136.

LVI
[to the Surveyor General]

Newmillerdam
July 20th 1803

Sir,

It is with great Reluctance I presume again to trouble you about the Execution of our new Lease; but really am compelled to do it by the repeated Importunity of my Co-Lessees, who have many of them expended considerably more than their own Fortunes in the Undertaking, and are still called upon for additional Sums of Money to perfect and support it: Since the last Account delivered in of our Expenditure, two more large Barns have been built, and another new Farm House is found necessary to be erected. I will beg Leave then to submit it to your own better knowledge and Understanding, how far we are entitled to all the Security in your Power to grant to us. I will however use one Argument more, and wch. I think will weigh forcibly with you; I mean the absolute Necessity there is of restraining the Tenants by the Penalties of a Lease from injuring the Banks, by making Roads over them etc; several Abuses of wch. Sort I have witnessed to my great Mortification.

I felt great Pleasure in being assured by Mr. Hiley Addington then Secretary to the Treasury, "that the Lords highly approved the Manner in wch. we had carried the Covenants of our Lease into Execution"; and trust therefore that your Kind Endeavours to serve us will meet with no Opposition from them. I will only add, that it shall be our constant Study to deserve any Encouragement granted to us.

I should not perhaps omit mentioning to You, that I opened our New Chapel sometime ago, and have appointed a Minister to perform Morning Service there every Sunday: You will believe it was no unpleasant Sight to observe a very respectable Congregation assembled there on the Occasion.

I will venture to indulge the comfortable Hope that you will soon give Instructions to Mr. Harrison for the Execution of our Lease; and that you will make our Covenant as favorable to us as you reasonably can.

I am with great Respect, Sir,
Your obed. Servant
J. Lonsdale

LVII
[to Harrison]

Newmillerdam,
Aug. 15th 1803

Dear Sir,

I am favored with your Letter[142] informing me, that the Surveyor General has now given full Directions for the completion of our Lease. With Respect to Mr. Marris's Statement of the respective Shares in our Petition for a Renewal of our Lease, if it was delivered in after our Arrival in London, I do not know of any Alterations to be made in them, except my own Purchase of Mrs. Foss's Share being one Twelfth, and wch was made for me by Mr. Marris previous to our entering on the Embankment: what I mean by this is, that Miss Foss died a little before that time, and by her Death one Twelfth came to Mrs. Lonsdale, and another was divided among the Welchs, Epworth, and Horton; and if this was not noticed before, it ought to be so now.

You will see then, that Mrs. and Miss Foss are to be left out of the new Lease. My own and Son's original shares of two sixths, together with Mrs. and Miss Foss's two Twelfths, make up to me and my Family one Half of the Island. But to prevent the Possibility of any Mistake, I will direct our Agent in Hull, Mr. Jackson to send to you an Account of the Shares as now rec^d. by the several Lessees.[143]

---

[142] This letter has not been found.

[143] The statement sets out the proportionate shares of the lessees in both 1797 and 1803 as follows:

1797		1803	
John Lonsdale	1/6th	Mr. Lonsdale	3/12th
Elizabeth Foss	3/12ths	Lonsdale Junr.	2/12th
Alexander Johnson	1/6th	Mrs. Lonsdale	1/12th
(in trust for Mr. Lonsdale's son)			
Humphrey Outwith	1/12th	Humphrey Outwith	1/12th
Epworth et ux.	1/9th	Epworth et ux.	5/36ths
Ruth Horton	1/9th	Ruth Horton	5/36ths
Miller et ux.	2/8ths of 1/9th	Miller et ux.	5/144ths
Mr. G. Welch	1/8th of 1/9th	G. Welch	5/288ths
" Joseph Welch	1/8th of 1/9th	Joseph Welch	5/288ths
" Lovelace Welch	1/8th of 1/9th	Lovelace Welch	5/288ths
" Chas. Welch	1/8th of 1/9th	Chas. Welch	5/288ths
" James Welch	1/8th of 1/9th	James Welch	5/288ths
" H. T. Welch	1/8th of 1/9th	H. T. Welch	5/288ths

You wisely say nothing to me about the present very dangerous crisis,[144] but stick steadily to your own Concerns. On this steadiness I depend with great satisfaction, and hoping to hear from you soon again am,

Dear Sir

Yrs. very truly

J. Lonsdale

LVIII
[to the Surveyor General]

Newmillerdam,

Feb. 28th 1804

Sir,

I take the earliest Opportunity in my Power of acknowledging the Favor of your communication to me,[145] and of assuring you, that Mr. Outwith and myself are ready to acquiesce in the Terms proposed to us for our new Lease, as far as we are able to perform them.

The additional yearly Rent of 40£ for every Acre of the old Land being plowed, and also the further additional yearly Rent of 10£ for every Acre of the new Land not managed and cultivated according to the Rules of the Lease during the last five years shall be chearfully complied with.

I enclose according to your Direction an accurate Valuation of the Buildings, and our Idea of the Sums to be insured on them; supposing in Case of Accident by Fire the Bricks and Materials saved to be of such a Value, as to make it unnecessary to ensure to the full Amount; And we are inclined to hope that the Buildings being new, and covered only with Tile, and being most of them detached from each other at very considerable Distances, the Danger of suffering materially by Fire will be greatly diminished. But we will leave the Sum most proper for our Insurance entirely to your

---

The changes are due to the distributtion of Mrs. Foss's quarter share amongst the other lessees, one third to John Londale, one third to Elizabeth Lonsdale, and the remaining third divided between the other lessees apart from Outwith whose share remained unaltered.

[144] Presumably a reference to the resumption of war with France and Napoleon's invasion preparations.

[145] No copy of this letter has been found.

Judgement. An additional new Farm House has been lately erected.

I opened the Chapel myself last Spring, and the Duty has since been performed there once every Sunday by a Clergyman from Hedon. But as such a Convenience may not always exist, and as very bad Roads in Winter, or deep Snows, will sometimes prevent an Attendance, we will agree to the Payment at least of the annual Stipend mentioned in the Draft of 21£.

I think your Objection to the Repetition of white crops[146] a very judicious one, and we will endeavour to avail ourselves of it, as much as we can; but our Agreement at the time with our Tenants was made was according to the usual and best known course of Husbandry in Holderness. If you think proper to send us a Field Book, we will enforce it as much as we can; and shall think ourselves obliged to you for any Directions you may think useful for the further Improvement of the Island.

But I am sorry to come to the last and I fear impracticable Part of your Proposals to us; I mean "the planting of Quicksets of White Thorn in such Parts of the Hedges and Fences as require the same". There are no Hedges upon the Island, the Inclosures being separated only by broad Ditches, cut to a proper Depth for that Purpose, and for holding Water in dry Seasons taken thro' the Cloughs. The Situation has been always considered particularly unfavorable to the Growth of Quicksets, arising as is supposed, from the Excess of Salt in the Land. There are no Quicksets planted in Mr. Constable's Estate[147] nor in the Lands belonging to the Sons of the Clergy; so that we are induced to hope you will not place us under any strict Covenant for this Purpose.[148]

Having now I think, gone through the principal Parts of the Draft I will trouble you no more than to request you, for myself and Co-Lessees, to grant us every Indulgence you think we may deserve, and to give your Directions for the Lease to be immediately proceeded on, our own Tenants being extremely impatient for having their Underleases executed as soon as possible.

---

[146] White crops are defined in a covenant in the lease as wheat, oats, barley, rye, hemp and flax. Two such crops were not to be grown in succession without a grass crop or ameliorating crop intervening to be eaten or consumed on the premises.

[147] Cherry Cobb Sand.

[148] The lessees were granted this exemption.

Mr. Outwith desires to join me in respectful Compliments to you, and I am,

Sir,

Your most obed^t. Servant
J. Lonsdale.

LIX
[*to Harrison*]

Newmillerdam,
March 5th, 1804

Dear Sir,

In my letter to the Surveyor General I omitted to mention the following Particular, but which I am sure you will have the Goodness to lay before him. In reading over the Draft of our intended Lease Mrs. Lonsdale could not help taking Notice of her own Name not being mentioned with the other married Women interested in it, but as our first Share in Sunk Island was left to Elizabeth Lonsdale by the Will of Mrs. Gylby, tho' not independently of her Husband, I shall esteem it a Favor done to me by the Surveyor General if he will permit her Name to be inserted.[149]

I am dear Sir,
Your obliged Servant,
J. Lonsdale

LX
[*to the Surveyor General*]

Newmillerdam,
March 12th 1804

Sir,

In the letter I had lately the Honor of addressing to You, I assured You, that Mr. Outwith and myself very readily assented to the increased annual Rent of £40 for every Acre of old Pasture Land ploughed and converted into Tillage.

We supposed it to apply only to old Land, wch shall be plowed up *after* this time; and tho' the Penalty be very great, yet having no Intention of ever incurring it, it did not appear to us of any

---

[149] This was done.

Consequence how great the Prohibition was: It might perhaps be less obnoxious to the Undertenants, and I hope too equally effectual, if the sum was reduced to £20 or £30.

But there is a Circumstance I now feel myself bound in good Faith and Duty to mention to you, tho' it did not strike me as necessary at the time of my sending our Answer to your Letter. It is this: When we first laid out the Farms on Sunk Island, there was a Surplice [sic] of inferior Grass Land of about 40 or 50 Acres not necessary for the Accommodation of any of the Principal Tenants. We therefore thought it best to erect our Cottages there, allotting to each a small Quantity of Land, and at the earnest desire of the Parties permitting them to plow a couple of Acres each for their own use and Subsistence. The Superintendant and Carpenter had of course a few Acres more than the Rest, and wch indeed we found necessary to obtain their Residence on the Island. They are however only Tenants from Year to Year and removable at Pleasure. Now I cannot but flatter myself that this Arrangement will meet with your Approbation and Concurrence when you consider the Necessity for it, and the Advantages it is calculated to produce on the Estate. If you think we have shown too much Indulgence, I will faithfully promise you, that the Portion of Grass Land plowed up shall be immediately laid down again in the most proper and husbandlike Manner. I beg of you to excuse this repeated Application to you, and am with great Respect,[150]

Sir,

Your most obed^t Servant,

J. Lonsdale

---

[150] The lease expressly extends the £40 penalty to "every acre of land ... which consists of old enclosed meadow or pasture land ... which shall be at any time ploughed broken up or converted to tillage or garden ground".

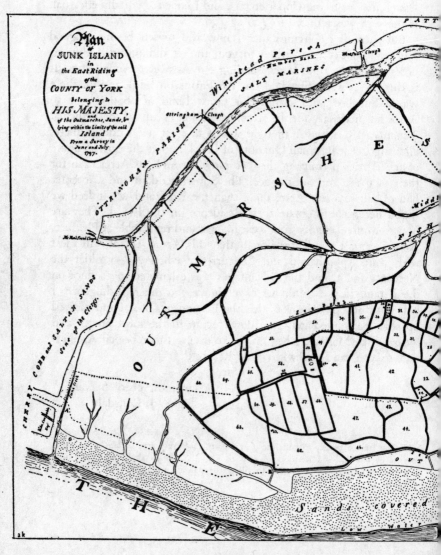

Facsimile of Whitelock's plan of Sunk Island made to accomp

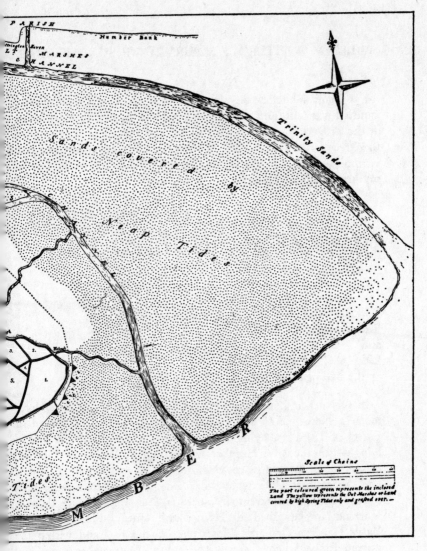

ey. The original measures 32¾ × 18 inches (83 × 45.5 cms).

WILLIAM WHITELOCK'S SURVEY OF SUNK ISLAND

I William Whitelock do swear that the Survey or Account hereto
annexed was faithfully and impartially made by me; that the Value
of the Property of the Crown therein contained is justly estimated
therein according to the best of my Skill and Judgement and that
all the Particulars stated in the said Survey are true to the best of
my knowledge and belief.

So help me God.
William Whitelock

Sworn at Ferrybridge in the County of York the twenty fifth day of January 1798	before us Hawke B. Frank B. Brooksbank

Yorkshire East Riding and Lincoln County or the one of them	Sunk Island in the River Humber

In Obedience to the annexed Warrant and Instructions, I have
taken a New Survey and Admeasurement of the said Island or
Parcel of Land belonging to his Majesty called the Sunk Island
lying within the River Humber in the County of York and Lincoln,
or one of them, now in possession of the Reverend John Lonsdale
and others their Undertenants or Assigns; and I have from such
Survey and Admeasurement caused a Plan to be made thereof,
whereon are described all Houses and other Buildings and all
Yards Gardens Orchards Closes and Parcels of Land within the
present Embankment thereof, And also all Outmarshes Sands and
other Lands without the present Embankment, but within the
Limits of the Island, And I have delineated in the said Plan all
Creeks Havens or Bays Pools or Ponds of Water, and all Banks
Drains Sluices Cloughs Jetties and other Works for embanking

and draining, and all Ways in and over the same, and the lines of the High and Low Water Marks, and of the Holderness Shore bordering upon the said Island. And I have further in obedience to the said Warrant and Instructions, made out the following Particular of my said Survey.

Present Names of the Tenants	No. of Reference to the Plan	Names of the Premises	How cultivated 1797	Quantities in each parcel A R P	Annual Value per acre	Amount £ s d
Missᵣˢ Harland and Lorryman	1	New Intack	Pˢ	66 1 0	28/-	92 15 0
	2	Part of dº	Pˢ	17 0 11	25/-	21 6 6
	3	Dan Creek or Sheep Walk	Ar	19 1 31	16/-	15 11 0
	4	,, ,, ,, ,, ,,	Ar	4 0 5	18/-	3 12 6
	5	,, ,, ,, ,, ,,	Pˢ	33 3 35	16/-	27 3 6
	6	,, ,, ,, ,, ,,	Ar	50 3 28	20/-	50 18 6
	7	Dan Creek	Water	3 2 39	—	— — —
	8	Dan Creek or Sheep Walk	Pˢ	21 2 18	18/-	19 9 0
	9	,, ,, ,, ,, ,,	Mᵈ	20 0 33	18/-	18 3 9
	10	,, ,, ,, ,, ,,	Ar	43 3 6	21/-	45 19 6
	11	,, ,, ,, ,, ,,	Ar	23 0 12	16/-	18 9 3
	12	Creek	Water	1 0 13	—	— — —
	13	Dan Creek or Sheep Walk	Ar	6 3 17	12/-	4 2 3
	20	Eighteen Acres	Pˢ	21 1 3	22/-	23 8 0
	21	Sixty Acres	Mᵈ	17 0 21	22/-	18 16 9
	22	,, ,,	Pˢ	57 0 37	25/-	71 10 9
	23	Home Close	P	23 3 15	25/-	29 16 3
	24	Hall Garden Court and Fold		4 0 37	—	5 0 0
		Road from the Hall to No. 14		1 3 8 ⎫		
		,, ,, ,, No. 6		0 3 8 ⎬	5/-	16 3
		Between Nos. 20 and 23		0 2 32 ⎭		
				439 0 9		466 18 9
		Outmark at the East end of the island		234 0 25	4/-	46 16 6
			acres	673 0 34		£513 15 3

Names of Tenants	No. of reference to The Plan	Names of the Premises	How cultivated 1797	Quantities in each parcel A R P			Annual Value per acre	Amount £ s	
Jere: Matcham	14	Low Close	Mᵈ	10	0	28	10/-	5	1
	15	,, ,,	Pˢ	8	0	5	8/-	3	4
	16	,, ,,	P	10	2	21	8/-	4	5
	17	Creek on West side of dº	Water	—	—	32	—	—	—
	18	Eighteen Acres	Ar	10	3	13	18/-	9	15
	19	,, ,,	M	8	3	24	20/-	8	18
	25	Great Close	Ar	15	2	—	18/-	13	19
	26	Squire Close with the Homestead	P	10	1	9	15/-	7	14
	27	Pingle	Pˢ	1	0	6	12/-	—	12
	31	Great Close	Ar	18	0	28	18/-	16	7
				93	3	6		69	17
		Outmarsh north of his Homestead		241	1	31	2/6	30	3
			acres	335	0	37		£100	0
Edward Coates	28	Far Close	P	7	3	—	14/-	5	8
	29	Middle Close	P	9	3	4	10/-	4	17
	30	Near Close	P	10	1	38	10/-	5	4
	32	Corn Close	Ar	14	2	2	17/-	12	6
	33	,, ,,	Ar	9	3	33	12/-	5	19
	34	Coppice with Barnard Fold	—	2	—	24	10/-	1	1
	35	Black Croft	M	2	2	22	18/-	2	7
	36	Home Close with House and Garden	P	9	—	8	20/-	9	1
	37	East Home Close	P	11	—	—	18/-	9	18
	38	Meadow Close	M	17	2	33	18/-	15	18
	39	West Close	Ar	20	1	6	18/-	18	5
				115	1	10		90	8
		Outmarsh north of the Homestead		196	—	—	4/-	39	4
			acres	311	1	10		129	12

Names of Tenants	No. of reference to The Plan	Names of the Premises	How cultivated 1797	Quantities in each parcel A R P	Annual Value per acre	Amount £ s d
Mr Stubbin and Mrs Roper	40	Bell Pasture	Ar	54 3 19	23	63 2 0
	41	,, ,,	Ar	42 — 36	22	46 9 0
	42	,, ,,	P & A	73 2 16	22	80 19 0
	43	Twelve Acres	P	12 3 24	25	16 2 6
	44	Decoy Close	P	54 3 14	20	54 16 9
	45	Creek adjoining	Water	2 3 36	—	—
	46	Thirty Acres	P	28 1 20	20	28 7 6
	47	Fourscore Acres	P	76 3 10	25	96 0 3
	48	House and Garden	—	1 17	—	1 0 0
	49	Corn Pasture	Md	9 2 2	21	9 19 9
	50	Corn Close	P	27 2 9	18	24 17 0
	51	Warren	P	38 3 17	22	42 14 9
	52	,,	P	7 1 36	22	8 4 6
	53	Barn, Stable, Fold, & Croft	P	8 1 21	15	6 5 9
	54	North Leys	Ar	48 — —	20	48 0 0
	55	Shepherd's House and Garden	—	— — 16	—	1 0 0
	56	South Leys	P	30 3 18	25	38 11 9
	57	Leys Close	P	29 — 4	23	33 7 6
	58	,, ,,	P	30 2 —	21	32 0 6
	59	,, ,,	P	27 3 20	21	29 5 3
	60	South Leys	M	14 1 14	21	15 1 0
	61	Clough Piece	P	1 17	10	— 2 9
	62	Old Intack	P	78 — —	23	89 14 0
	63	Shepherd's Cottage and Garden	—	— — 23	—	1 5 0
	64	Middle Intack	P	85 3 17	22	94 8 6
	65	North Leys	P	20 2 21	20	20 12 6
	66	Warren	P	4 — 18	18	3 14 0
	67	West Intack	P	57 1 37	21	60 7 0
	68	,, ,,	P	43 1 31	21	45 12 0
		Lane between 49 and 52		0 2 30		
		,, between 40 and 56		— 2 12		
		,, from No. 52 to 67		2 1 4		
				912 3 29		992 — 6
		Outmarsh exclusive of Creeks		2492 1 29		200 — —
		Creeks in D°		44 0 16		— — —
			acres	3449 1 34		£1192 0 6

The foregoing Farms collected

Tenants	Within the present Embankment Quantities in A R P	Ann. Value £ s d	Without the present Embankment Quantities in A R P	Ann. Value £ s d	Totals Quantities in A R P	Ann. Value £ s d	Present Rent in £ s d
Messrs Harland and Lorryman	439 0 9	466 18 9	234 0 25	46 16 6	673 0 34	513 15 3	500 0 0
Jere Matcham	93 3 6	66 17 0	241 1 31	30 3 6	335 0 37	100 0 6	90 0 0
Edward Coates	115 1 10	90 8 9	196 0 0	39 4 0	311 1 10	129 12 9	110 0 0
Mrs Roper and Mr Stubbing	912 3 29	992 0 6	2536 2 5	200 0 0	3449 1 34	1192 0 6	1120 0 0
Totals	1561 0 14	1619 5 0	3208 0 21	316 4 0	4769 0 35	1935 9 0	1820 0 0

Sands to Low Water Mark

	A	R	P
Sands partly covered at the time of Neap Tides			
North and East of Fisherman's Channel	19	1	0
Due South and West of said Channel	32	0	24
Sands covered at Neap Tides North and East of the said Channel to Low Water Mark	2920	0	15
Other Sands South and West of D° to Low Water Mark	1588	0	8
Fisherman's Channel from Letter D to Low Water Mark	103	2	16
	4663	0	23
Brought down	4769	0	35
Total acres	9432	1	18

BUILDINGS

The Buildings are in general indifferent and insufficient for the accommodation of resident Tenants. Mr Harland lives at Burton Pidsey, and Mr Lorryman at Tunstal. The House on their Farm is usually called the Mansion House built of Brick and covered with Tile and Lead, it contains a Dining Room of Deal Wainscot, an Inner Closet or Parlour, a Front Parlour, Back Parlour and Dairy but without Chambers over them. The Offices are now used as Labourers Houses, one consisting of Kitchen Parlour and Small Pantry, with two Chambers over the Kitchen and Parlour, and another of Kitchen, Back Kitchen, Parlour and Small Pantry with one Chamber over the Kitchen and Parlour, a Stable for Six Horses, with a Hay Chamber over it, and on the back of the Stable, a Shed for the standing of Six Cows: A Barn four Bays in length, all of which Offices Stable Shed and Barn are built of Brick and covered with Tile and in fair Repair. The Mansion part of the buildings is in bad repair and uninhabited, except one Room used as a School for the Labourers Children, who in July last were ten Boys in Number. The Roof, Ceilings, Windows and Doors, have been much neglected and going fast to ruin.

Jeremiah Matcham's House consists of a Kitchen, Back Kitchen, Parlour and Dairy with two Chambers, built of Brick and covered with Tile, is small but in fair repair. The Barn is only three Bays in length and low, built of Brick and covered with Thatch. This homestead is in want of a Stable and Cow House, having only bad temporary Hovels for Draught Horses and Milch Cows. Jeremiah Matcham is the only resident Tenant.

Edward Coates lives at Ottringham, the House on his Farm is of the same dimensions and materials as Matcham's House, and is in good repair. The Barn and Stable are detached from the House, the former is small, being only three Bays in length and low built of brick, and covered with Tile, the latter is in a good new Building of Brick and Tile for Six Horses or Cows.

Mrs Roper and Mr Stubbings live at a distance—their Farm

House consists of Two Front Rooms, a Back Kitchen, Brewhouse and Pantry or Dairy, with three Chambers, is built of brick and covered with Tile. The Outbuildings are a Barn of five Bays in length, a Stable for Eight Horses and Standing for Four Cows, also of Brick and Tile, and in Fair Repair.

In No. 55 is a Shepherd's House of low Rooms and Two Chambers, and in No. 63 is another Shepherd's House of like dimensions built of Brick and Tile and in good repair.

The Farm Folds are only fenced in a temporary Way with Posts and Rails, and sheltered with Stubble.

The Gates are in general good Repair and the Bridges. The Island is inclosed by a Bank and Drain and subdivided by Fence, Ditches and Drains, which have three Outlets at H, I and K to which are proper Cloughs or Sluices to let off the Water and prevent the Tide Water returning upon the Island, these are also in good repair, but the Jetties and Works necessary for protecting the Island from Wear or Waste by the Humber at G and I have of late years been neglected and a large quantity of Whitecliff Stone[151] is immediately wanted for the purpose, and I estimate that under the present mode of letting and management of the Island that a Sum of not less than £550[152] is now requisite for the necessary additions and Repairs of Buildings Repair of Jetties and formation of New Ones and that a Sum not exceeding £100 per Annum would be sufficient to keep them in repair.

Neither Soil or Situation are adapted for the growth of Timber. Mr Gylby formerly a Lessee of the Island planted a number of Trees for ornament in Nos. 24 and 34, and there is now remaining in the former place (to the front of the Mansion House) Ninety-eight Elms, and three Ash Trees; Twenty-three of the Elms are worth upon an average five shillings each and the remainder 1/6d each; in a Balk or Grass Verge West of the House are thirty small Elms, and in the yard East thereof Forty of a stinted growth and of little or no Value. And in No. 34 are One Hundred and seventy one small Trees alike stinted in their growth; three of which are Oak worth 2/6 each, Twenty Ashes worth 1/6 each, and the rest Elms worth on an average 6d each. These Plantations have been

[151] i.e. blocks of chalk from the quarries by the Humber at Hessle, four miles west of Hull.

[152] Should be £650 vide estimate Page 18. [i.e. p. 150. This correction is in the original MS].

neglected of late years and are exposed to the depredations of Cattle or otherwise would not only have been ornamental, but would have afforded much shelter.

There are no Commons; nor is the Island subject to any Claim of Common Rights. There are no Mines, or Quarries within the Precincts of the Island; The Warp or Clay thereon is fit for the purpose of turning into Brick but from which no other advantage can be derived than for the purpose of Materials for any New Erection or Repairs of the present or future Buildings.

Fisherman's Channel being nearly in the Center of the Island is considered an exclusive Property belonging to His Majesty, but the liberty of Fishing has never been refused to the Fishermen of Pattrington, and without their paying any acknowledgement. This, with the circumstances of an Embankment herein proposed of the Outmarshes, which would most probably be the means of causing that Channel to Warp up, induces me to consider the Fishing of no Annual Value.

Sunk Island is extraparochial and Tithe Free; it maintains its own Poor; and the rate on that Account is now about £25 per Annum, and paid by the Tenants. The Land Tax amounts to £43 4s annually but although considered as part of and nearest adjoining to the East Riding of the County of York pays no County Rate or Quit or other Rent, or Outpayment whatsoever save an annual reserved Rent to His Majesty of £80 1 8d and £5 5s per Annum to the Sons of the Clergy, for the privilege of a Road by Saltah Grange and which is said to be fixed by an Act of Parliament passed for the division of Cherrycob Sands. These last several payments together with Repairs of Banks and Jetties are allowed by the Landlord.

There are now seven resident Families upon the Island, two on Messrs Harlands and Lorrymans, one on Jere: Matchams, one on Edward Coates's and Three on Mrs Ropers and Mr Stubbing's Farms and the number of Persons Men, Women and Children are from Thirty to Forty, the Number in each Family varies in the Seasons according to the want of Labourers in the management of the Farms.

The Chapel which was formerly built by a Mr Gylby of Lincoln was after the death of the late Mr Gylby neglected and became ruinous and totally taken down six years ago. The Reverend Mr Pearson late of Kayingham was the last Minister who performed

Divine Service there, and who had done so Thirty years,—once a month in the Summer Season and once in Six Weeks in Winter, at a Salary from the said Mr Gylby of Fourteen Guineas per Annum, and Provision for himself and Horse, but it does not appear from any Account I could procure that the support of the Chapel or expenses of the Minister were otherwise than voluntary on the part of the Lessees.

Pattrington and Headon are the two nearest Market Towns, at the distance each of ten Miles by the present Road which in both instances are by Kayingham, and Saltah Grange. Pattrington is a Mile from the Haven, which is divided from the Island by the North Channel, and can only be passed by Boats, no communication however has hitherto been attempted by that way between the Island and Pattrington because of the long track of Marsh, intersected with Creeks laying between them, it may however, and probably will be used as a means of communication with Pattrington, whenever these Marshes are embanked and the North Channel will be a means of conveying off a part of the produce of the Island, as well as bringing Lime and Coal for the use of the Farmers, and the Fisherman's Channel is now partially used for those purposes, as well as the River Humber from the South West Point of the Island.

The common mode of cropping the Arable Land in Sunk Island, is Fallow, on which they sow Cole or Rape Seed for the Winter and Spring Feed of their Sheep this is succeeded by Oats, Wheat, Beans, and then Fallow again, and which I conceive to be the best in this Instance. It appears from the Particulars of the Survey that the proportion of Arable to Grass Land (within the embanked part of the Island) is as one to three, and which ought not to be increased until there are more Inhabitants, for although the Land is well adapted for the growth of Corn, it is also equally well adapted for the breed and feed of Cattle and much extra expence and inconvenience for want of Inhabitants, is and would be experienced in Weeding, Reaping, Housing and Converting the produce of a Corn Farm in this particular situation. The produce it is true may easily be taken to Market by the River Humber and the North and other Channels, but I cannot on that Ground only advise the permission of a greater quantity being converted into arable than now is, and the Tenants should be bound down to it by Covenant and not to be permitted to plough out any ancient Sward without leave, and that at the discretion of the Landlord, on their first having laid down to Grass in a Husbandlike manner an equal quantity; and they should be bound to keep the Buildings, Fences, Banks, Drains, Gates, Bridges, Cloughs and Jetties in good Repair and Condition, and for want of such Repairs, that the Lessor have power to enter, do them and be repaid by an additional Rent to be recovered in the same mode as other Rents are recoverable.

I have also further in obedience to the said Warrant and Instructions proceeded by taking into consideration what part of the Outmarshes are capable of being embanked and inclosed with advantage to the Undertaker and the mode and expence thereof and of draining and taking off the Water not only from the said Outmarshes, but also from the inclosed part of the said Island, and am of opinion that the greatest part of the said Outmarshes within the

                                        A   R P

dotted Lines A, B, C, D, E and F, and containing 2714 2 27 are of that description and that as His Majesty, his Lessees and the Community may and will be greatly benefitted by the Undertaking, it is a thing highly eligible and ought to be done.

The present Drainage for the inclosed part of the Island is at three Sluices or Cloughs marked H I and K emptying their Waters from thence through Creeks in irregular courses to Fishermans Channel and of course the preservation of the Drainage depends upon the Fishermans Channel being kept open or adopting a new Outfall. It is found in the Memory of Men living that Fishermans Channel has been in a progressive way of warping up, and John Salisbury an Old Fisherman of Pattrington who remembered it much larger (is an instance) and who also believes it will in time totally warp up. This is likely. For the only Security of keeping a Channel open through a long flat Shore, and of such Material as this is composed of depends upon a constant run of fresh Water, and which cannot be the case in Sunk Island, as there is no run of fresh water but in Wet Seasons, besides a diversion of the Outlet will most probably by a means of Silt or Warp laying up quicker at the East End of the Island, and of course the gain of more Land to His Majesty and Lessees.

By the Scheme of a projected Embankment herein set forth, a Delf or Excavation for the Bank on the inside would answer the purpose to lead to a new Outfall into the North Channel, but as the Projectors for an improvement of the Holderness Drainage are proposing, instead of the Water passing through North Channel (because their Water has been found insufficient to keep that Channel properly open) to turn a part by way of Headon and the remainder by Cherry Cobb Sands to Stone Creek, and into the Humber near the Letter G and being there within a quarter of a Mile of Low Water Mark, and deep Water in the Humber, I think, that place would be the best Outfall for the Drainage of the whole Island, and not only by being so near Deep Water but also the space between Deep Water and the Shore having a good chance of being kept open by the Scouring of the Holderness Water.

Estimate of the Expence of Embanking Drainage and other Requisites for the Improvement of 2714 2 27 of Land part of the Outmarshes of Sunk Island.

	£	s	d
To a Bank of Ten feet in Perpendicular height, and on a Base of Fifty feet on the side next the Humber from A to B 1½ miles and 16 Chains	1122	0	0
To a Bank of Nine feet in height and on a Base of Forty five feet on the East Side from C to D and E. 2½ Miles and three Chains	1319	2	6
To a Bank of Eight feet in height and on a Base of Forty feet on the North Side from E to F two miles and nineteen Chains	945	2	0
To filling up Creeks in the way of Embankment	681	15	0
A Sluice of Stone with eight Feet Water Way	800	0	0
	4867	19	6
Incidents 10 per Cent.	486	16	0
	5354	15	6
A Main Drain of 120 Chains in length and 24 feet Top by Stone Creek and to Fisherman's Channel	277	15	0
Fencing into Sixty four Pieces with ten feet Ditches or Drains will (besides taking in Creeks that will serve as Fences) be in length 1622 Chains	655	7	6
Sixty four New Fence Gates Posts & hanging	80	0	0
Ten Carriage Bridges	60	0	0
Forming four Miles of Road	63	0	0
Immediate Repairs of Jetties	350	0	0
Three New Homesteads not less than	1800	0	0
Repairs and necessary additions to the Old Ones	300	0	0
Total	£8940	18	0

Note: In the heading above the estimate, "A R P" appears centered over "2714 2 27".

Estimate of the Annual Value of the Outmarshes when so taken in and improved on a Lease of 31 years.

	Quantities	Ann. Value per acre	Amount		
	A R P		£	s	d
A R P Of the 2714 2 27, I estimate that the Drains and Roads will take up a Quantity of Land not less than	43 3 36				
There are in Creeks and other Wastes a part of that gross quantity	45 1 39				
And of Land fit for the purpose of cultivation	2625 0 32	15/-	1968	18	0
	2714 2 27				
Will remain without the proposed Embankment against North Channel taken up by the Excavation, Bank and Foreshore which will on an Average be worth 3/- per Acre	62 2 24	3/-	9	7	6
On the South side of Ropers and Stubbings Farms	204 0 28	5/-	51	0	0
On the South side of Harlands and Lorrymans	83 2 16	7/-	29	5	0
More on South Side of the said two Farms covered by Neap Tides and on which is little or no Herbage	18 2 12		—	—	—
On the East side of the propsed Embankment of inferior quality but will be worth 2/- and may in time be much more	124 1 34	2/-	12	8	6
Total Acres	3208 0 21		£2070	19	0
All which Outmarshes in their present State are rated at			316	4	0
Clear Annual Improvement			£1754	15	0

From all of which I infer and humbly certify that in my opinion for the

	£	s	d	
inclosed part of the said Island	1619	5	0	and
for the said Outmarshes when Embanked	2070	19	0	

Together   3790   4   0   is a

fair Annual Value thereof Out of } which I deduct the Land Tax }   43   4   4

Way Leave by Saltah Grange   5   5   0

The Repairs by Sluices, Banks and } Jetties because of great extension } together with Repairs of Buildings }   200   0   0

                                 248   9   4

Clear   £3441   14   8 to be

let on a Lease for the Term of Thirty one Years, to commence from the Time of the Embankment Drains, Buildings and Fences being completed.

William Whitelock
Brotherton, 24th January 1798

To John Fordyce Esq }
Surveyor General of His }
Majesty's Land Revenues }

INDEX OF NAMES

INDEX OF PLACES

MISCELLANEOUS